Customer Empathy

A radical intervention in customer experience management and design

Alex Allwood

ALL
WORK
TOGETHER

For Mum
1934–2019

Customer Empathy
A Radical Intervention in Customer
Experience Management and Design

First published in Australia in 2019 by
All Work Together (Australia) Pty Limited
Level 8, 99 Elizabeth Street, Sydney, NSW, 2000
allworktogether.com.au

ISBN: 978-1-925921-65-6

A catalogue entry is available for this book from
the National Library of Australia

Cover design: Adrian Checkley
Editing: David Thompson
Internal design and book production: Michael Hanrahan Publishing

Contents

1
Prologue

How would you feel, if every time you contacted your bank they addressed you by the wrong name? And even though you explained that this wasn't your preferred name, they said, "Sorry that name's in our system, and it can't be changed". How would that make you feel?

My expectations aren't unrealistic—with most companies I buy from I can use my preferred name. Even with countless satisfaction surveys completed, nothing has changed. The feeling I get, is this business doesn't care. My relationship does not feel good.

Performance reports from Forrester, KPMG Nunwood and Qualtrics XM Institute, reflect current customer experience (CX) practices are failing organisations and their customers. For organisations around the world the returns from investing in customer experience excellence are not being fully realised.

Forrester's Customer Experience Index showed again this year that CX excellence remains elusive for the majority of businesses, as "81% of brand scores stagnated; most industry front-runners were repeats; many gains too minor to render them statistically significant."[1]

Qualtrics XM Institute's global report produced by Bruce Temkin surveyed 212 organisations with annual revenues of $500 million or more. The findings show only 6 percent of companies have achieved top level CX maturity; the majority, 79 percent, remain low in maturity.[2]

Organisations have bought into the promise of enhanced customer value, competitive differentiation and CX as a driver of sustainable growth. However, with the exception of 100 or so high-performance, leading brands such as Airbnb, Amazon, Disney, Sephora, Slack, Warby Parker, Zappos and the like, the rewards remain elusive.

For twenty years now, organisations have worked at developing their customer-led cultures; appointing a senior CX leader and dedicated team, developing CX strategy, investing resources into measuring customer satisfaction, mobilising teams to operationalise improvements, reorganising teams to work in new ways and innovating customer touchpoints.

Despite these resources, efforts, and insights gleaned through advanced technologies and data analysis, still "only 14 percent of marketers say that customer centricity is a

---

1   forrester.com

2   qualtrics.com

hallmark of their companies, and only 11 percent believe their customers would agree with that characterization."[3]

Why, with so many organisations investing vast amounts of energy and effort into customer experience excellence, is there at best, only incremental gain? What's missing from current customer experience management and design practice that's impeding progress? How might we change the status quo to benefit customers, employees and businesses? Something is missing.

As it stands, customer experience management and design is overdue for radical intervention.

In my work as a customer experience management consultant I have observed a fundamental CX practice gap—an empathy deficit. I am experiencing this deficit in my consulting with business leaders and their teams, in my customer experience training, in conversations with colleagues and through the evidence presented in published research and articles. This empathy deficit is perpetuated through the perceived low value of empathy as a skill, a shortfall in empathetic leadership, a siloed mentality within organisations and an obsession with customer satisfaction scores, to name just a few.

Customer empathy is understanding your customer's perspective, feeling what they're experiencing and

---

3   D. Lee Yohn, '6 Ways to Build a Customer-Centric Culture', hbr.org, October 2, 2018

considering this in your decision making. Switching on and strengthening the ability to empathise provides a new lens through which to see the customer's world differently through perspective-taking. Empathy provides meaning for what's important in designing and delivering customer experiences. Critically, empathy is fundamental to customer centricity; putting customers' needs at the centre of thinking, problem solving and decision making.

Customer empathy is a powerful human resource for positively impacting customer experience excellence that until now, has been largely overlooked.

In findings from a 2015 Global Empathy Index report, "the top 10 empathy performers generated 50% more earnings than the bottom 10, while average earnings at the top were up 6% this year whereas they dropped 9% at the bottom, and if we look at just the top 5, we see year-on-year market capitalization growth soaring at 23.3%, compared to an average 5.2% across the Index as a whole."[4]

So what does customer empathy at work look like? When I first spoke with the senior leadership team of a large company in the tourism sector, they were doing CX by the book; using the right business, customer and social metrics and employing this data to solve customer touchpoint problems using technology. They wanted to understand why these improvements hadn't been as effective as expected.

---

4   B. Parmar, 'Which companies are best at empathy?' weforum.org, December 3, 2015

"We want to start by mapping the journey," they said to me. "Let's start by talking with your customers," I replied. One executive vocalised his objection, "We already know our customers' problem from the CSat—it's queuing!" Fair comment, their customers were obviously very vocal about queuing. In social media, many customer comments were along the lines of, "Love this place, but they should do something about the lines!"

Nevertheless, we moved beyond satisfaction surveys to first-hand conversations with customers. Putting aside our assumptions to learn about the customers' world and understand how they felt, what they were thinking and why; this was a game changer.

Viewing their customers' interactions through the lens of their experiences, it became crystal clear that queuing per se wasn't the root cause of poor experiences. Instead, it was the specific stresses associated with queuing. This was the 'ah-ha' moment. The one-on-one conversations provided the context to identify and understand the core of the problem.

For employees of this business, their customers' stories evoked real emotion. Storytelling and showing, using customer thinking and feeling, had a profound effect on them. They leant into the journey map that stretched along the walls. Huddled in small teams, reading and discussing the verbatim comments aloud; tracing their fingers over the emotion graph to feel what customers were feeling.

For many the 'light went on' through understanding the experience from their customers' perspective, instead of making assumptions based on their own truths. Most were enlightened and felt empowered to make a difference—and there were a few that found the process understandably confronting.

This is customer empathy at work—understanding the customer's perspective, feeling what they're experiencing and considering their needs in the decision making process. Empathy played an important role in connecting teams emotionally with the work that needed to be undertaken to reduce queuing stress—prioritising this work over competing initiatives.

Deeply understanding their customers' experience—from their customers' point of view was the catalyst for change. Their focus shifted to augmenting satisfaction scores with customer conversations, moving from touchpoints to customer journeys, combining customer emotion with behavioural insights and engaging in customer needs-based problem solving and decision making.

As the founder and principal consultant for All Work Together, I have the privilege of working with leading Australian and international organisations, helping them to connect customer and culture; empowering leaders and employee teams to work together to enhance customer value and drive customer-centric growth. I also enjoy teaching people in business how to develop and strengthen their customer empathy skills.

Whilst I don't describe myself as an empath, I still have the ability to feel what another person feels; I'm well-attuned to other people's emotions. Some years ago I had my personal strengths analysed and my top strength is strategic. I was a tad disappointed empathy didn't feature, however it was what the strengths coach said that surprised me: "We've identified 32 human strengths and in your case, if strategic is your top strength, empathy is your last."

In light of this assessment I've worked to switch on my empathy ability; practising the skills of empathetic listening, keeping an open mind and suspending judgement, and sharing my understanding of another's perspective. Developing my empathy muscle has improved my thinking, problem solving and decision making.

Customer Empathy has been written with the express aim of humanising current approaches to customer experience management and design. The ability to empathise enables us to see the customer's world differently. Through feeling their emotions and understanding their perspective we create more meaningful connections, align and unite teams and enrich our decision making to make a difference in customers' lives—and in doing so, deliver customer experience excellence.

2
Decoding Empathy

"She looks forward, her brow raised with concern and her hands clasped. She's not speaking and doesn't show any sign that she is about to launch into a political speech. She is simply listening."[1]

This is the face of human empathy. The image of Jacinda Ardern, Prime Minister of New Zealand, circulated around the world, making global headlines and appearing in every social media feed. In a world where terror and trauma dominate our daily news feeds it resonated strongly with people everywhere.

As her country mourned in the aftermath of a deadly terrorist attack, her words, "they are us", brought everyone together as one; united in universal human values. It was a sentiment reminiscent of her earlier, debut speech to the United Nations General Assembly where, "She asked for

1   G. McConnell, 'Face of empathy: Jacinda Ardern photo resonates worldwide after attack', smh.com.au, March 18, 2019

leaders to 'step back from the chaos' and find a sense of simplicity, to be guided by one concept—kindness."[2]

Ardern embodies human traits seldom seen in high profile leaders today; she exudes qualities that are defining a different type of leadership, one of optimism, inclusion, equality, communication openness and most of all, empathy.

What is empathy?

Empathy is understanding another person's point of view, feeling what another person is experiencing and considering this in your decisions. Empathy can be explained as the ability to feel and share emotions; and the ability to match another's emotions. "Empathy seeks information about another and helps us understand their situation, whereas sympathy reflects actual concern about the other and a desire to improve their situation."[3]

Empathy is often interchanged with sympathy or compassion. Sympathy is responding to suffering with pity or sorrow, whereas compassion is the awareness of another's suffering and the desire to respond with an act of kindness or care. This differs from empathy, which includes the ability to feel a range of emotions, including happiness. Some academics argue that sympathy and compassion are responses to empathetic concern.

---

2   S. Sachdeva, 'Ardern advances a kinder worldview on world stage', newsroom.co.nz, September 28, 2018

3   F. de Waal, *Mama's Last Hug*, London: Granta Publications, 2019, p. 106

Empathy expert, Dr. Helen Riess, describes empathy as when, "We temporarily imagine someone else's thoughts and feelings and experience their discomfort. Typically, this leads to *empathic concern*, a caring feeling toward another person that motivates a compassionate response."[4]

Riess explains in her book, *The Empathy Effect*, that different people are moved in different ways and at different times to care. It could be a small act of acknowledgement, such as a warm hello to someone down on their luck, helping someone who's tripped over or simply being present when you're listening; these acts of care and compassion are motivated by empathetic concern.

Daniel Goleman, psychologist and author of *Social Intelligence*, categorises empathy as not a single trait, but one of three. The first of these, Cognitive Empathy, is the ability to understand another's perspective. The skill of comprehending another person's point of view which requires having a mental grasp of their view, attitude or opinion.

The second type of empathy is Emotional Empathy, the ability to feel what another is feeling, as if their emotions were contagious. Emotional Empathy is being well-attuned to another person's emotions. When that now famous image of Prime Minster Jacinda Ardern appeared in newsfeeds across the world—we all deeply felt her sadness, through the expressions on her face, her body language and the way she clasped her hands.

---

4   H. Riess, MD, *The Empathy Effect*, Boulder: Sounds True, 2018, p. 9

The third type is Empathetic Concern; this is the type we most often associate with when we hear the term empathy. Empathetic Concern is understanding, feeling and sensing what we need to do to help another person; it's empathy in action. Goleman describes this as the ability to sense what another needs from you and to respond with sympathy or compassion.

On the day after the New Zealand terrorist attack, in an unprecedented action, Jacinda Ardern responded with empathetic concern. She demonstrated understanding, compassion and solidarity with New Zealand's Muslim community by wearing a hijab. Her actions showed her fellow New Zealanders and the world that being empathetic is a powerful leadership quality.

When we utilise empathy in our interactions with others, we engage with them through empathetic listening; asking questions and having an open mind that's free from judgment—setting aside our own assumptions about their lives to gain real insight into their needs. When we interact with empathy, we use verbal acknowledgements and non-verbal behaviours including facial expressions, eye contact and body language; we communicate that we recognise and understand their perspective.

Emotional consciousness

Empathy enables us to connect human to human; it feeds our interest in each other—as much as we try, we can't help but be affected by another's emotional state. "Our empathic connection with others is like an under-the-table handshake between bodies, perceived as a 'vibe' which may be positive and inspiring, or toxic, sapping our energy."[5]

The German psychologist Theodor Lipps inspired the term empathy when he was watching a high-wire act. Lipps noted that when watching the performance, it was as if the viewers emotionally entered the high-wire artist's body, sharing his experience, as if they were on the tight-rope with him.[6]

I've recently had a similar experience. At the time, I was coaching startups in Service Design practices. Equal Reality is an Australian company that specialises in Virtual Reality (VR) corporate diversity and inclusion training and their team was prototyping a new training module.

With the VR headset on I selected an avatar: female, twenty-five, height 160 centimetres. I walked into the virtual meeting room and was introduced to the very tall and titan-like, all-male virtual team. I felt rather over-whelmed. I looked up at them and I felt quite small and inconsequential; my voice softer and more feminine, and with less authority in this virtual world. I realised that this is how many women experience their working lives!

Powered by empathy our emotions literally jump from one person to the next! "… by unconsciously becoming one with another's body, we gain similar experiences,

5   F. de Waal, *Mama's Last Hug*, London: Granta Publications, 2019, p. 88
6   Ibid

feeling their situation as if it's our own."[7] We experience this with the urge to yawn when another is yawning, we smile at people who smile at us, we feel happy when we're around positive people and when others cry, we cry too.

Mirror neurons

Research suggests that empathy is hardwired into our brains. As discussed, empathy encompasses comprehending another's perspective, feeling their emotions and sensing the care that's needed. Empathy experts believe "... neurological 'mirrors' and shared circuits give us the ability to *understand* not just what another is thinking but to *feel* what they are feeling as well."[8]

It was a group of Italian researchers working with primates that discovered mirror neurons. Interested in how the brain works, neurophysiologists Giacomo Rizzolatti, Giuseppe Di Pellegrino, Luciano Fadiga, Leonardo Fogassi, and Vittorio Gallese, examined the brain activity of macaque monkeys; when a monkey picked up an object, the computer recorded the animal's brain activity.

One day, when Fogassi had walked into the lab and picked up a peanut, he observed that the monkey's brain neurons lit up the same way as when the monkey performed this action itself. Intrigued, the researchers ran further experiments with other objects. In each case, the

---

7   Ibid, p. 94

8   H. Riess, MD, *The Empathy Effect*, Boulder: Sounds True, 2018, p. 9

monkey's brain reacted as if the monkey was performing the activity.

The scientists named their discovery 'mirror neurons' because they enable us to replicate in our own mind what others are doing. That is, the same area in the brain lights up whether the action is performed by the individual themselves or that individual is observing another person performing the action. This discovery sparked an explosion of neuroscientific studies, which has led to the belief that shared neurological circuits enable us to understand what others are thinking and feel what others are experiencing too.

A recent study by Michael Kraus, Yale University School of Management, found that our hearing may be stronger than our vision in detecting emotion. Kraus found that people focus on listening to the way a speaker expresses themselves. "When you are speaking to someone on the phone, for example, you might be more likely to notice if they are breathing quickly and appear nervous, or if their speech is monotone and they sound down or tired. On the other hand, you can easily detect enthusiasm and excitement when someone speaks in a high-pitched and rapid manner."[9]

Another study has found that when two people speak with each other and understand each other, "Their brains literally synchronize. It is as if they are dancing in parallel,

9   E. Seppala, 'Does Your Voice Reveal More Emotion Than Your Face?' greatergood.berkeley.edu, June 19, 2017

the listener's brain activity mirroring that of the speaker with a short delay."[10] Empathy involves understanding the emotional states of other people—and it is our expression of emotions and feelings that communicates this to each other.

Empathy face

Humans are built to relate to each other. Our facial expressions help us connect with each other by mimicking expressions. By subtly mirroring another person's facial expressions we understand what they are experiencing.

Clinical psychologist Paul Ekman is renowned for his research into facial expressions and their relationship to basic emotions. He discovered facial expressions of emotions such as joy, fear, anger, sadness and surprise were universal, and these expressions could be easily read across all peoples and cultures.

In his latest book, *Mama's Last Hug*, primatologist and ethnologist, Frans de Waal explains that emotions are as much a part of the body as they are of the mind. Emotions are "mental states that make our hearts beat faster, our skin gain colour, our faces tremble, our chests tighten, our voices rise, our tears flow, our stomachs turn, and so on."[11]

---

10   E. Seppala, 'Does Your Voice Reveal More Emotion Than Your Face?' greatergood.berkeley.edu, June 19, 2017

11   F. de Waal, *Mama's Last Hug*, London: Granta Publications, 2019, p. 84

Think of emotions as mental and feelings as physical—we know when we are angry because we feel it. De Waal explains the connection between emotions which can be automatically triggered, and feelings "arise when emotions penetrate our consciousness, and we become aware of them."[12]

Most of us are capable of reading other people's expressions to understand what they're thinking and feeling. Many studies show that empathy gives us the ability to read other's emotions by mirroring or mimicking their facial expressions, tone of voice and body language. It is mirroring that helps to facilitate empathy, understanding what another is experiencing through reading their human expressions.

Interestingly, but not surprisingly, a study by David Neal and Tanya Chartrand, published in *Social Psychological and Personality Science*, showed people using Botox to smooth their facial 'expression lines' (wrinkles) are unable to imitate the facial emotions of other people—using Botox decreases a person's ability to empathise with others. "It's no shock that we can't tell what the Botoxed are feeling. But it turns out that people with frozen faces have little idea what we're feeling, either."[13]

Botox freezes their facial muscles, thereby robbing them of the ability to mirror facial expressions, reflect

---

12   Ibid, p. 87

13   P. Paul, 'With Botox, Looking Good and Feeling Less', nytimes.com, June 17, 2011

emotions and connect with the feelings of another. Their facial unresponsiveness can leave them feeling emotionally disconnected or even rejected. The problem is not only how they relate to others, but also how others relate to them. Botox inhibits them feeling what others are feeling.

Walking in my shoes

Jane Elliott is a teacher, lecturer and trainer, and recipient of the National Mental Health Association Award for Excellence in Education. In response to the assassination of Martin Luther King Jr., Elliott devised the 'Blue Eyes/ Brown Eyes Exercise'. This now famous exercise labels participants as inferior or superior based upon the colour of their eyes and exposes them to the experience of being in a minority.[14]

A school teacher at the time of King's death, Elliott asked her students if they wanted to learn what racism felt like, and developed the exercise to help the kids walk in another person's shoes. The idea of 'walking a mile in someone else's shoes' is the perfect metaphor for explaining the concept of practicing empathy.

Over the following weeks Elliott's students were divided into blue-eyed and brown-eyed groups. The blue-eyed group was labelled smarter and cleaner; the superior group. The exercise taught the children a powerful lesson about the experience of being considered superior or

---

14   janeelliott.com

inferior because of a trait that you can't control, and how discrimination and racism feel at first hand. The kids discovered how it feels to be in another person's shoes and what the experience of others is *really* like.

So what are experiences really like for your customers?

Most executives and employees do not know what it feels like to be a customer of their business. They believe, because of their industry expertise, or because they've purchased a like-product and are customers themselves, or because their customer feedback score provides enough insight, that their assumptions of what the experience feels like for customers is enough to make the right decisions; forging ahead without considering the very people they're endeavouring to make a difference for—their customers.

3
Customer Empathy Deficit

I will never forget the day when United Airlines passenger, Dr. David Dao, was knocked unconscious and forcibly dragged off his flight. Like millions of others, I watched in disbelief as a customer who had paid for his ticket was hauled out of the plane for refusing to give up his seat on the overbooked flight.

His violent removal past rows and rows of distressed passengers was captured by fellow passengers on their mobile phones—one video was "shared over 87,000 times and viewed 6.8 million times"[1] in less than 24 hours. It took United's CEO, Oscar Munoz, three tries before his public apology statements showed any empathy.

Munoz's first statement of apology was appallingly low on concern: "I apologise for having to re-accommodate these customers."[2] Again, social media went into meltdown. In his second statement, Munoz compounded his

---

1   United Express Flight 3411 incident, en.wikipedia.org

2   P. Gourguechon, 'Empathy Is An Essential Leadership Skill – And There's Nothing Soft About It', forbes.com, December 26, 2017

error by blaming the victim, describing him as, "defiant, belligerent and disruptive."[3] Only on his third attempt, when Munoz said, "I promise you we will do better"[4] did he demonstrate any empathy for customers, employees and a horrified public.

In the weeks that followed the Dr. Dao disaster, there were successive incidents on United flights. In one, a flight attendant insisted a passenger's pet dog travel in the overhead luggage compartment, and despite assurances that the dog would be fine, the customer's pet was found dead upon arrival.

United's empathy deficit reflected a poor company culture and poor leadership. Allowed to thrive, this poor conduct flourished; it proliferated and was rewarded. Even with a mandate from Munoz to empower employee decision making, to 'put customers first', the airline's relentless focus on efficiency and operationalisation of policies was so entrenched, that employee capacity for empathic concern was suppressed.

Losing customer connection

Organisations face a seemingly insurmountable challenge in transitioning to a customer-centric culture. Executives and employees alike have lost their human connection

---

3   P. Gourguechon, 'Empathy Is An Essential Leadership Skill – And There's Nothing Soft About It', forbes.com, December 26, 2017

4   Ibid

with customers. They have lost a propensity to understand customers—to perspective-take, to step into their customers' world and experience their lives from the customer's point of view; to understand how their customers think, feel and experience.

Instead, employees are bound to their work through technology, data, scores and business outcomes. Organisations too, are structured to deliver greater productivity and efficiency, increasing internal competition and decreasing collaboration and communication. In consequence, businesses' thinking, problem solving and decision making have become less and less human. Without customer empathy, how do we bring organisational understanding and meaning to what's important to customers in designing and delivering experiences?

Author of *Wired to Care*, Dev Patnaik, describes corporations as like a building; bringing people together, protecting them from the world and providing them an environment in which to work effectively. "When you're inside a building with central heating and cooling, the temperature is perfectly tuned to be pleasant … it also cuts you off from clues about the weather outside."[5] As a metaphor this aptly describes the status quo in many organisations— employees are starved of customer perspective, which leads to customer understanding deprivation and a lack of empathetic concern.

---

5   D. Patnaik, *Wired To Care*. New Jersey: Pearson Education, 2009, p. 131

Many leaders see empathy as a soft skill and 'fluffy'. Compared to other highly regarded leadership traits such as endurance, efficiency and effectiveness, empathy is grossly undervalued. Empathy is often viewed as being a weakness, too emotional when 'emotions have no place in business'. When, for example, was the last time you saw empathy as a required skill in a recruitment ad? To their detriment, organisations haven't considered customer empathy as a commercial tool or as an employee skill; one that can be switched on, developed and strengthened.

Empathy and power

United Airlines' Oscar Munoz has admitted the airline's relentless focus on efficiency created a toxic culture that forced employees to prioritise efficiency over their care for customers. "We let rules and procedures get in the way of our people."[6] This had resulted in customers experiencing poor employee behaviour, poor leadership decision making, an ongoing lack of judgement, rudeness, and a perception of incompetence. Munoz's leadership had prioritised business gain at any cost.

Research shows that personal power interferes with a business leader's ability to empathise. Dacher Keltner, social psychologist at the University of California, Berkeley, has conducted studies showing "that people who have

---

6   O. Staley, 'United's CEO admits the airline had an unhealthy obsession with rules', qz.com, June 19, 2018

power suffer deficits in empathy, the ability to read emotions, and the ability to adapt behaviors to other people."[7] Keltner argues, "It's more common to see leaders fail in the area of every day self-management—and the use of power in a way that is motivated by ego and self-interest."[8]

Interestingly, those who hold the seats of power in organisations tend to come from similar backgrounds. They attended the same schools, live in the same suburbs, lead the same lifestyles, have risen up the management ranks together and are well remunerated for their experience and expertise. As they climb up the corporate ladder, organisational leaders look less like their customers—less like ordinary people.

Leaders have become disconnected and out of touch with their customers—living their lives in a bubble. Rosemary Sainty, UTS Business School academic and founding Australian representative to the UN Global Compact, believes there is a systemic lack of leadership empathy with customers. Sainty argues directors have little understanding of customer needs. "They don't know them. How can they act in their best interests?"[9]

Richard Boyatzis, professor at Weatherhead School of Management, Case Western Reserve University, argues that

---

7   L. Solomon, 'Becoming Powerful Makes You Less Empathetic', Empathy (HBR Emotional Intelligence Series), Boston: Harvard Business Review Press, 2017, p. 64

8   Ibid

9   S. Patten, 'Clubby directors in 'bubble of sweet content' have no understanding of customers', afr.com, December 5, 2018

"lack of empathic concern in organisations results in multiple disasters, including losing touch with the hearts and minds of your staff, your customers, your suppliers and community. It goes hand in hand with a lack of moral concern, resulting in decreased activation of the brain's default mode network, the part of the brain that's active when a person is thinking about others, remembering the past and planning for the future."[10]

Empathy lost in silos

Organisations are plagued with silos; operational silos, channel silos, system silos and data silos—large businesses need silos or specialist departments or teams to get work done. Organisational structures use functional silos in an effort to reduce complexity and promote efficiency and productivity; decreasing costs and increasing output to maximise shareholder returns—mostly at the expense of customer experience.

Organisational silos reflect an employee's specialist classification and expertise, and there's little reason to disrupt the functional group they've been assigned to. The reality is, the employee siloed mindset is entrenched in most organisations. Evidence of the siloed mindset is seen in a 'them versus us' attitude, job demarcation, or situations where employee teams are crippled; stifling productivity,

---

10   H. Riess, MD, *The Empathy Effect*, Boulder: Sounds True, 2018, p. 148

blocking coordination of resources and effort and negatively impacting the delivery of customer experiences.

Departmental silos have their own goals, incentives and agendas. They often have a limited customer view and a limited understanding of, or interest in, customers. Instead, their primary focus is product/service-centric or serving internal stakeholders. Silos perpetuate a culture of competitiveness, defensiveness and tribal discord, resulting in inward-looking departments and blinkered decision making.

For CX efforts, the siloed mindset impacts customer collaboration; stifling a unified and coordinated approach on customer experience effort. Turf wars commonly perpetuate the hoarding of information in silos; information impacting the availability of critical data and insights for problem solving and decision making. Silos create bureaucracy, are the death of effective CX management practice and the cause of customer infuriation.

Customer empathy gets lost in functional silos; suffocated by a culture of unsympathetic behaviours, where employees lose touch with customers' needs in the grind of day-to-day competitive business pressures. As the author of *The Silo Effect* Gillian Tett argues, "when our classification systems become excessively rigid, and silos dangerously entrenched, this can leave us blind to risks *and* exciting opportunities."[11]

---

11   G. Tett, *The Silo Effect*, New York: Simon & Schuster, 2016, p. 247

Empathy's number is up

Organisations have an unhealthy data obsession. The volume, velocity, and variety of data is overwhelming, to the point where customers are, more often than not, expressed as a number; a satisfaction score, a data point, sale, account number, revenue or profitability metric etc. Our fixation with data, metrics and more recently, performance-related customer scores, is stifling empathetic concern for customers.

Customer satisfaction metrics, such as Customer Satisfaction scores (CSat), Net Promotor Scores (NPS) and Customer Effort Scores (CES), were intended to rally employees to improve customer experiences. Instead, an obsession with score chasing is having the opposite effect. While some organisations use customer experience metrics well, many more are choosing to focus efforts on measurement over systemic change to improve end-to-end experiences.

A recent article in *The Wall Street Journal* on score obsession argued, "Management consultants are notorious for pushing ideas to CEOs using jargon and claims of improved business performance. NPS has outlived such fads, spawning a cottage industry of consultants and software firms that help businesses implement and boost their score."[12]

---

12   K. Safdar and I. Pacheco, 'The Dubious Management Fad Sweeping Corporate America', wsj.com, May 15, 2019

Instead of employee focus on improving customer experiences, reward and incentivisation for score improvement is driving effort towards attaining a good score result—a score 'lift'. In the worst cases I've seen, employees are biasing surveys by selectively targeting customers who will give a good score, priming surveys with specific language and even pressuring customers for higher ratings.

Fred Reichheld, the inventor of NPS, said he is " astonished companies are using NPS to determine bonuses and as a performance indicator. That's completely bogus. I had no idea how people would mess with the score to bend it, to make it serve their selfish objectives."[13]

Reinforcing this view, motivational researcher Carol Dweck and behavioural economist Dan Ariely have observed, "Employees end up spending a lot of energy on improving a score, and it's never a great customer experience when somebody begs you for a 10. More importantly, score-obsessed employees are highly likely to become cynical and lose the sense of pride in their work, which is a sure way to destroy any chance of becoming a customer-centric organisation."[14]

Layer upon layer, organisations are building systems with the aim of delivering business performance at the expense of improving customer wellbeing. Systems that keep customers at arm's length and promote employee

---

13   Ibid

14   M. Schmidt-Subramanian, 'Customer-Obsessed Companies Embrace Metrics Differently', cmo.com, November 21, 2017

behaviours that develop empathetic detachment, individualism, ego and self interest. Data now represents customers that are out of view, who are seen as scores rather than human beings, disconnecting employees from the purpose of their work—to make a difference in customers' lives.

3 core skills to develop and strengthen customer empathy

Customer Empathy

Storytelling

Listening

Curiosity

© Alex Allwood

4
Listening with Empathy

During his presidency, Barack Obama received an average of 10,000 letters every day. When Obama incorporated the ritual of listening to 'the people's voice' into his demanding daily schedule, his actions sent a clear message to the White House—the people we serve, the American public—their lives matter. To understand their lives and their needs, we need to listen to their stories.

From this simple step of listening, Obama demonstrated what he valued, 'the people's voice', his constituents. Obama didn't mandate his daily listening practice across the White House. This wasn't a forced regime. Instead, he led with his actions, with what was in his heart. He "brought a solid well of empathy to the office"[1] and demonstrated empathy through his everyday behaviours.

---

1   J. M. Lakas, *To Obama, With love, joy, hate and despair*, London: Bloomsbury, 2018, p. 343

Through his empathetic leadership style constituency listening became a priority; part of the White House's culture.

Fuelled by constituent empathy, Obama's behaviour became contagious across the White House and 'the people's voice' became just as important to his advisers, policy makers and staff. They explained that reading the letters became like nourishment for them. In the Obama White House, empathy through listening became what Malcolm Gladwell would describe as a 'Tipping Point', "that magic moment when an idea, trend, or social behaviour crosses a threshold, tips, and spreads like wildfire."[2]

Listen to grow

Being customer-centric is the practice of putting customers' needs at the centre of your organisation's thinking, problem solving and decision making. The first principle of customer centricity is listening to customers. Listening with empathy meaningfully connects employees with customers' lives.

Customer listening tells an organisation what they're doing well, where improvements can be made, and where opportunities exist. Listening informs improvements in experiences, new ways of doing things, solutions that make customers' lives easier, undiscovered market opportunities

---

2   M. Gladwell, 'The Tipping Point', gladwell.com

and signature brand experiences—all of which can deliver greater value for customers, competitive advantage for the business and new ways to drive growth.

Empathetic or active listening begins with being interested in your customers' lives; what's important to them, their struggles, and the problems they're trying to solve. In my work I've listened to first-hand customer stories of queuing in forty-degree heat, patients dying in waiting rooms, essential services being cut during billing disputes, 100 percent increases in licensing costs, petrol tankers bursting into flames, fraudulent tax activity and customers begging for their calls to be returned. These are my clients' customers' stories—their courage to actively listen with an open mind and share these customer stories with humility across their business demonstrates the essence of customer empathy.

Active listening is a key skill in exercising empathy to understand your customer's perspective. This is a different type of listening to what's typically found in organisations. This is first-hand conversations to learn about customers, their culture and their context, through their stories. Many executives confuse active listening with market research; asking questions about what customers like/don't like/want to turn their feedback into new product or service features. It's also not the same as using a Voice of Customer (VoC) survey to gather customer satisfaction feedback.

Listening with empathy requires developing new skills and practices to proactively promote and scale executive and employee participation; so that customer empathy becomes an integral part of a business's everyday behaviour. Barack Obama's presidential leadership listening became a beacon for change; a strong signal for what was important. Reading constituent letters became a contagious ritual throughout the White House; connecting the White House 'business' and its employees (both traditionally disconnected and physically removed from the citizens they served) with improving citizens' lives.

Measuring satisfaction

In their efforts to provide better experiences for their customers, many organisations have now incorporated a Voice of Customer (VoC) feedback program into their operations, with the aim of using customer feedback surveys and satisfaction scores to measure and understand their organisational performance.

Voice of Customer is a term that describes customer feedback about their experiences with a company. Typically, VoC is measured using Customer Satisfaction scores (CSat) and/or Net Promotor Scores (NPS) and sometimes Customer Effort Scores (CES). Scores, however, underrepresent customer listening because there's very little or no customer emotion connected with these numbers.

The score represents satisfaction with a group of brand interactions, likelihood to recommend, or customer effort.

The challenge with scores like these, is making this data meaningful for employees. Usually shown as an infographic within a dashboard, these scores represent a metric which reflects how well the business has performed in delivering their products and services. Whilst this metric has a role to play, it doesn't explain to employees the 'why' behind the score.

To try and overcome this problem, organisations have incorporated comments sections within their surveys. Asking respondents, 'Why did you give us this score?', can help to provide customer experience context, however, without sophisticated text analytics to synthesis insights, collecting feedback data in this way is a pointless exercise.

Empathetic ear

Deep customer understanding comes from a multi-layered listening approach that incorporates first-hand customer conversations with solicited customer feedback (VoC). Think of a multi-layered customer listening approach as a three-tiered cake.

The top layer of the cake represents customer satisfaction scores. The second layer is customer verbatim feedback and the bottom layer is the foundation. The foundation must be 'empathic listening' or 'active listening'; first-hand customer conversations using contextual enquiry research or in-depth, one-on-one customer interviews.

Empathetic listening starts with being curious and interested in customers' lives. The problems they are trying to solve, the jobs they're trying to get done and their experiences; their feelings when they are interacting with your products and services.

Being active in listening is being present and attentive. Observing your customer's facial expressions and body language, acknowledging and asking the right questions at the right time and importantly, setting aside your own assumptions to gain real insight into your customer's needs.

"When you listen with an empathic ear, you call upon many empathic keys. With your ears, you take in not just the word, but also the prosody and tone. With your eyes, you watch the person's face and body language. You draw upon your instincts and your 'heart' to uncover the emotional intent behind the words."[3] As you're listening, you should be asking yourself, 'What must this feel like?'

Being empathetic in your listening helps you to understand the message your customer is sharing and keep track of the points made in the conversation. People who are effective at listening with empathy remember what's being said and will reference these points in their follow-up questions, which assists in building trust and rapport.

Unlike VoC data, these first-hand conversations enable customers to share their point of view and express their

---

3   H. Riess, MD, *The Empathy Effect*, Boulder: Sounds True, 2018, p. 56

feelings; especially their frustrations, which helps organisations identify the root causes of customer problems. Empathy expert Dr. Helen Riess's research shows that "paying attention to the problem at hand only gets you so far. Paying attention to the underlying issues that people deeply care about is where the golden experience of mutual empathy and understanding comes together."[4]

How to actively listen

It still surprises me that most people in business, employees and executives alike, have never spoken with a customer—ever! They have never taken or been offered the opportunity to understand their customer's perspective—and herein lies the challenge in developing a customer-centric culture.

In my customer experience training workshops, many attendees share their nervousness at the prospect of having an in-depth, one-on-one customer conversation—they tell me for example, that they 'wouldn't know what to ask'. Some (usually junior managers) are anxious about saying the wrong thing. However, just by listening to customer conversations, hearing their perspective in their own words, helps you step into the customer's world.

---

4   Ibid

When I work with employees to improve their customer conversations, I start by emphasising the importance of being present; being attentive, interested and curious to learn something new; having a learner's mindset, observing non-verbal cues such as facial expressions, gestures, body language and tone of voice.

As discussed in the earlier chapter Decoding Empathy, a study by Michael Kraus, Yale University School of Management, found that our hearing may be stronger than our vision in detecting emotion. "Kraus found that we are more accurate when we hear someone's voice than when we look only at their facial expressions, or see their face and hear their voice."[5]

Being mindful of your own presence is the best place to start. I suggest practising active listening at home with your partner or in the office with colleagues. Use a video to capture your body language and facial expressions; are you relaxed and at ease or intense and intimidating? Are you being present and attentive or distracted by a notification on your mobile phone? Are you being interested in the points being communicated and incorporating these into your follow-up questions to build trust and rapport?

User researcher and author Steve Portigal says, "If your brain is listening your body will naturally follow.

---

5   E. Seppala, 'Does Your Voice Reveal More Emotion Than Your Face?' greatergood.berkeley.edu, June 19, 2017

But it works the other way too!"[6] Acclaimed journalist and author Malcolm Gladwell elaborates, "Emotion doesn't just go from the inside out. It goes from the outside in… In the facial-feedback system, an expression you do not even know that you have can create an emotion you did not choose to feel."[7]

As countless studies show, when we have a conversation we can't help but unconsciously imitate the other person's expressions; using all of our senses to detect their emotions; mirroring their facial expressions, body language and tone of voice. Empathy helps the listener understand the meaning of what's being said and what the other person is feeling—this is empathy at work!

Listening from the top

When the IBM board appointed Lou Gerstner to turn around the ailing company in the 1990s, he named his listening initiative 'Operation Bear Hug'. Gerstner realised that the business's experience alone was not enough to turn IBM around—and he saw listening as an important step in the strategy-creating process. Over three months he met with employees and customers to ask about the challenges they were dealing with, and how IBM could help.

---

6   S. Portigal, Interviewing Users, New York: Rosenfeld Media, 2013, p. 26
7   Ibid

Gerstner also requested his 200 direct reports meet with customers to listen to their feedback and directed each of them to write a report to be submitted directly to him. Gerstner read every one. He called customers every day. He listened, put his assumptions to one side and tried not to draw immediate conclusions.

"That empathic connection to real-world customers helped managers to see whether a particular decision added value for customers or destroyed it."[8] Operation Bear Hug led to quicker customer resolutions, new market opportunities and the transformation of an inwardly focused culture—all through asking the single most important question when people were making decisions and problem solving, "What are our customers telling us?"[9]

More importantly, Gerstner's customer-centric approach revealed some major opportunities, such as leveraging the power of the internet through e-commerce. His approach inspired IBM's cultural transformation from an internally focused, inside-out bureaucracy to a customer-led, outside-in innovator.

Scaling empathetic listening

Many of my contemporaries advocate customer listening through Voice of Customer; using solicited customer

---

8   D. Patnaik, *Wired to Care*, New Jersey: Pearson Education, 2009, p. 121
9   Ibid

surveys to scale customer feedback across their organisations. There are, however, many customer listening methods that scale empathetic customer listening to effectively promote deeper customer connection and understanding.

A great example is utilising customer listening immersion sessions for groups of employees. More of a longer conversation—like having a discussion with a group of friends—these sessions are powerful empathy builders, especially for non-customer facing employees and executives who have low-to-no physical connection with customers. During these sessions employees listen to customer's first-hand stories about their experiences; feeling what it's like to be a customer and hearing their point of view to better understand their perspective.

I heard another great example of customer listening when I was a panel moderator for Mumbrella's Finance Marketing Summit. Jane Merrick, the then GM Marketing and Customer Experience for IAG (of which NRMA Insurance is an operating group), outlined one of IAG's listening initiatives called 'Customer Connections', which included a group listening exercise at their annual conference. One hundred and fifteen senior leaders, who typically had low-to-no customer interaction, were asked to call customer advocates to say thank you for being an NRMA customer.

That day, 1,500 calls were made by the leadership group. "We had people that had worked there for a long period of time who have never spoken to a customer in really senior positions."[10] Many calls were to long-standing, loyal customers, some had been using NRMA for 40-50 years. "We made all these calls to the customers to basically say thank you and it was the first time some of them had heard from us…"[11] outside of delivering an insurance service.

From this initial listening exercise the business committed to rolling out a program across the organisation. "We started out just doing advocates because we wanted to just ease people into these conversations and then we will be moving onto detractors and passives as well."[12] For employees too, the experience of calling customers had far-reaching benefits, helping employees feel recognised for their involvement in providing their customers rewarding experiences.

Listening with empathy connects employees to customers' lives. For Barack Obama, his focus on listening with empathy was a core value of his presidency—part of his political philosophy, and connected to his early days of campaigning of "going around and listening to people. Asking about their lives, and what was important to them."[13]

---

10   alexallwood.com.au

11   Ibid

12   Ibid

13   J. M. Lakas, *To Obama, With love, joy, hate and despair*, London: Bloomsbury, 2018, p. 345

Obama believes everybody has a story, and "they're willing to share it with you if they feel as if you actually care about it."[14] Obama says of his dedication to listening to understand "this form of story sharing and empathy and listening … creates the conditions around which we can then have a meaningful conversation …"[15]

14   Ibid
15   Ibid, p. 347

5
Curious
to
Know

When I was thinking about this chapter, I reflected back to when I was a child. I was one of those annoyingly inquisitive kids that asked way too many questions. I googled this and found a study in the UK that showed curious children ask between 70 and 90 questions per day—I can only imagine that my parents found this exhausting!

It's no wonder then, that the only 'words of wisdom' I can recall in response to all my 'Why … ?' questions was, "Y is a crooked letter and you can't make it straight." So, I don't believe it's a coincidence that what I'm passionate about is understanding 'Why' and using this to solve big problems.

The creator of TED Conferences, Richard Saul Wurman, is obsessed with asking questions. He says that the idea of asking a good question, is asking the simplest question. "When you step on an ant and the ant dies, you say, 'It's dead, it's no longer here.' A four or five year old can say, "What's death? What's life?" It's a simple question but it's very complex."[1]

Author of *The Book of Beautiful Questions*, Warren Berger, makes the point that kids ask endless 'Why' and 'What if' questions—however they gradually ask fewer questions as they progress through school. By the time we start our careers "many of us have gotten out of the habit of asking fundamental questions about what's going on around us."[2] It's as though our childlike curiosity just disappears!

Learner mindset

Children can teach us a thing or two about how to learn. Our mindset is determined by the questions we ask. A person with a 'learner mindset' has an inquisitive approach to asking questions; open minded and creative—exploring possibilities that lead to discovery and understanding. An approach that asks questions with an attitude of openness and enthusiasm to learning something new, without assumption or judgement.

To get the right answers, you'll need ask the right questions. Albert Einstein once said, "If I had an hour to solve a problem and my life depended on the solution, I would spend the first 55 minutes determining the proper question

1   E. Robertson, 'Richard Saul Wurman, My World is a Lattice', the-talks.com, October 22, 2014

2   W. Berger, 'The Power of 'Why?' and 'What If?', nytimes.com, July 2, 2016

to ask, for once I know the proper question, I could solve the problem in less than five minutes."[3]

I couldn't agree more! Most of the time, we get fixated on the solution. We fall in love with our own ideas without exploring through asking questions the other ways of seeing the problem—then we ask questions to confirm our decision. For example, there's a big difference between 'We need to build a bridge' (the solution) and 'How might we cross the river?' (the question). The solution shuts down all of the possibilities for solving the problem differently.

To develop your customer empathy muscle, put your assumptions to one side. Most people find this challenging. What is helpful is to remind yourself to have an open mind, to actively listen and observe, but not to judge. Even when you think you know the answer, be curious, don't assume, ask a question—and listen with empathy to your customers to learn more about them and their world.

In having an engaging conversation with customers, you'll need to adopt a learner mindset, putting aside your own biases and suspending your assumptions and judgements. Our personal experiences, beliefs and frames of reference create assumptions which we use to make sense of the world we live in, however our assumptions and the judgments we make affect our ability to empathise.

---

3   W. Berger, 'Einstein and questioning: Exploring the mind of one of our greatest thinkers', amorebeautifulquestion.com

The challenge for us all, is given what we know, how do we take a fresh perspective? While reading Warren Berger's book, *The Book of Beautiful Questions*, I came across a reference to a well-known scene in the movie *Dead Poets Society*. In the movie, Robin Williams' character dares his students to stand on their desks, because "the world looks very different from up here."

Inhibitors in asking questions

Given as kids we do well at asking questions, we naturally assume that adults do too. Unlike the professionals such as reporters, doctors, police and counsellors, who are taught how to ask questions, most business people don't see asking questions as a skill that can or needs to be improved.

Research from Harvard Business School shows people don't ask questions for several reasons. In conversation, people can be egocentric; focused on sharing their thoughts and stories without considering the need to ask a question. They can be apathetic and don't care enough to ask, or they can be overconfident and think they know all the answers. Some people worry about being seen as incompetent by asking the wrong questions, "But the biggest inhibitor ... is that most people just don't understand how beneficial good questioning can be."[4]

---

4   A. Wood Brooks and L. K. John, 'The Surprising Power of Questions', hbr.org, 2018

I find this too, with participants in my customer experience training workshops; asking questions is their barrier to deeper customer understanding. Even with an interview guide prepared, most participants are weak in first-hand customer conversation skills; not asking the right questions to build the conversation and uncover valuable customer insights. To begin with, their discussions are generally quite short, lasting only ten to 15 minutes, and often they're unable to build their next question from the response given. They are surprised to learn that an in-depth customer interview will often stretch 4 to 6 times longer.

In these training sessions I am interested to understand their customer interviewing barriers. They often share with me an apprehension of being judged for asking too many questions, lack confidence in asking the right questions to deliver the right answers and generally feel uncomfortable because there's an awkwardness; a feeling of unease between them and the interview participant. The good news is, everyone experiences these feelings when they start to conduct first-hand customer conversations.

In the following pages I deep dive into first-hand customer conversations; how to build rapport to help your customer feel at ease and the types of questions to ask customers to understand their experiences. Whilst you or your team might not be ready to undertake customer interviews just yet, these next sections will aid in developing an interview guide.

Building rapport

Conversation flow comes from building the "deepest rapport … when the participant has spent enough time immersed in the topic in a supportive and explorative fashion."[5] Kick off an in-depth discussion by being human and making the customer feel at ease to build trust.

The other person is more likely to discuss in detail their experience if they feel relaxed in the discussion. Even if you don't naturally click and there's an awkwardness, I always try to find something that's interesting about them, such as knowing more about their background. Get curious about their story; your curiosity will shift your facial expressions and body language and change your intent; helping you to build empathy and better understand their experience.

Asking the right questions leads to conversation flow. It's the point at which the other person shifts from giving short answers to your questions, to telling their stories. In his book *Interviewing Users*, Steve Portigal describes this as "a point where you realise that you've arrived at a high level of rapport and the tenor of the exchange is different."[6]

At this time the conversation shifts from answering questions to sharing contextual information about themselves; their goals, motivations, beliefs, hopes and most importantly, their feelings. This is the point that

---

5   S. Portigal, *Interviewing Users*. New York: Rosenfeld Media, 2013, p. 80
6   Ibid, p. 79

you become drawn into the customer's world—living through their experiences, taking their perspective to see a new truth.

You're asking questions to better understand your customer's world and how they see it. The questions you're asking shouldn't be a line list of topics about your products, services and touchpoints; it's more a discovery process than a survey. A good way to think about your conversations is that an in-depth discussion is 'like going on a date'. When you're on a date, you're there to learn more about the other person and their life.

For this reason, I suggest to people that they write an interview guide for reference, rather than a Q&A checklist. The aim of the interview guide is twofold: to keep everyone in your team aligned and to gather information to understand the problems your customers are trying to solve.

These questions are often asked in a structured way; starting with general questions to build rapport, moving quickly to open-ended questions to explore a broad range of possibilities, then probing questions to fill in missing information and closing questions to end. I also recommend that interview guide questions are treated as fluid rather than fixed.

Interviews never happen the way you imagine, as you deep dive into your customer's world unexpected topics surface that can be explored and validated with successive customer interviews. What's important here is your conversation discovery is debriefed to your team, to allow them to explore this line of enquiry in their customer interviews.

Question types

Being empathetic in asking questions, results in a better understanding of how your customers feel about their experience. Your role is to be inquisitive and to explore the possibilities. This includes asking about the feelings associated with their experience. Emotions impact customer experiences—asking questions to learn 'why' they feel the way they do will help you to understand the root cause of customer experience motivations and problems.

Closed questions call for specific answers; usually a yes/no or one-word response. Closed questions are good for fact finding and easy for your customer to answer, however, they also can stifle conversation and are much better for confirming information than beginning a line of enquiry. A good example of a closed question is, 'Did you use our website to find out about our services?' Closed questions typically begin with: 'Are', 'Did', 'Do' and 'Is'.

Loaded or leading questions are another variation. You'll often see loaded questions in customer satisfaction surveys, such as, 'What did you like most about our service?' This line of enquiry is either loaded with assumption or asks a question with the answer already in mind—one that serves the questioner's agenda. The tip here, is don't risk biasing your research by assuming or influencing the customer's responses. Being curious to know, rather than making assumptions, helps build and strengthen your customer empathy ability.

Open-ended questions give you a chance to put your empathy listening skills into practice. These types of questions suggest to the other person that you want to hear what they have to say—that you want to learn about them. Open questions encourage the respondent to reflect on what's important to them. An example of an open question is, 'How did you find out about our services?' Open questions typically begin with: 'What', 'How', 'Show/Tell me' and 'Why'.

Probing questions are based on response and invite a deeper examination. These questions build upon previous answers, helping to uncover the reasons behind the responses. Probing questions ask for an example or to describe circumstances. Customer context makes the experience easier to understand. For example, 'Can you tell me more about …?' or 'How did that make you feel?'

I'm a fan of asking 'why'. A curious questioner asks the why behind the answer that's been given. If you want to get to the root cause or the reason, you'll need to ask why. Asking why helps uncover the emotional drivers behind the response. As discussed in Chapter 2, Decoding Empathy, most of the time we're not aware of our emotions and often people have trouble putting their feelings into words—unless there's a heightened emotional moment.

This is why asking 'feeling' questions is so critical. Asking 'feeling questions' provides understanding of the customer emotions associated with their experiences. When you ask about how they feel, they'll often provide a short answer such as, 'It made me frustrated.' Gentle, probing questions will help you understand what 'frustrated' really means to them in that context. For example, 'Can you tell me more about why this made you frustrated?'

As discussed in Chapter 4, Listening with Empathy, active listeners understand the message in the information that's being shared and keep track of the points made in the conversation. People who are effective at listening with empathy, remember what's being said and will reiterate these points in their following questions; continuing to building trust throughout the discussion. As you're listening, you're asking yourself, 'What must this feel like?'

Tempted?

It's often tempting to ask customers for solutions and ideas in your discussions. It might be suggested you ask customers how they might solve the problem or how they see the solution. For example, 'What should we do differently?' or 'How might we fix this problem?' Questions such as these only lead to mediocre ideas based on your customer's current state expectations. Whilst customers can tell you about the problems that they're experiencing, customers don't know what the solution is, because they view their ideas through the lens of their current experiences.

6
Storytelling and Showing

Recently, I've been working with a client's senior leadership team, one member of which hadn't shown an active interest in the work of improving experiences (more common when working with non-customer facing teams). While Tim (name changed) had 'walked in the customer's shoes' in an immersion workshop, he remained disconnected from the level of frustration customers were experiencing.

In the next workshop, I asked Tim to kick off our session by sharing a customer story; helping his fellow team members step into their customer's world. "No problem, I've got this," he said, as he walked confidently to the front of the room to address his colleagues.

Using the customer journey map to guide his story-telling, he walked us through the interaction highs and lows of the customer's product usage journey. Using customer language instead of business speak, he described their goals at each step and used their verbatim comments to describe how customers felt; referencing the emotion graph to show the range of emotions customers were experiencing through the various stages of their journey.

As he shared their stories, a noticeable physical change came over him. From a confident 'I've got this' demeanour to slumped shoulders, he started tripping over his words, his voice quietened and his delivery slowed. Everyone in the room felt this moment of realisation too, as he concluded his presentation by saying, "I had no idea our customer experience was so poor—I AM GUTTED."

Humanising scores

So much of our storytelling in customer experience management is through customer satisfaction scores. The challenge with scores alone, is the number only represents a fraction of potential customer experience data. The score only tells how the business has performed, which can lead employee teams to believe they have enough information to make good decisions.

Customer satisfaction scores have become a necessary evil; seen as a quantifiable measurement of customer experience performance. Typically, what's found on a CX report card is information on how the business is performing using satisfaction metrics such as Customer Satisfaction Score (CSat), Net Promotor Score (NPS) and Customer Effort Score (CES), and an outcome metric of performance against the customer actions such as sales figures, number of complaints or online reviews etc.

We must ask ourselves, are we too readily reducing our customers to just a number—or in customer experience measurement, a score? Many times I have had conversations about scores without ever discussing customers and their unmet needs; these conversations in organisations tend to lead to a culture of score obsession—getting higher scores becomes more important than a focus on making a difference in customers' lives.

Many of you will relate to this 'groundhog day' scenario. Scores are updated at the end of the week, the team then spends the next week searching for the explanation as to why the score had dropped by 0.5 points. Friday comes around again, the score is updated again and this time it's risen 1.25 points. So the hunt for an explanation for the previous week's drop stops in favour of an enquiry into the reason for the net gain … and so on and so forth.

Scores create a visibility gap. This customer visibility gap is a barrier to knowing, understanding and caring about customers. "We regulate empathy by opening or closing a door, depending on who we identify with and feel close to."[1] To understand customers, we need to develop meaningful connection by seeing, feeling and hearing them. "We need an individual object of identification, an actual body and face, to open the door to our heart."[2]

What the score doesn't tell is the customer story behind the score; how pre, during and post interaction moments

1   F. de Waal, *Mama's Last Hug*, London: Granta Books, 2019, p. 90
2   Ibid, p. 92

impact their experience. For example, the working, single parent who is unable to take the day off to wait for the internet technician, or the pensioner who can't afford to heat their home and is late in paying their electricity bill, or the spouse who prepares, cooks and delivers her sick husband's meals so he doesn't have to eat the food provided by the hospital.

Wired to Care author, Dev Patnaik makes a critical point about empathy too: "your mirror neurones do have one important limitation: they need first hand sensory input, they still require you to meet another person to understand what he or she is going through."[3]

Without context, immediacy, personal connection and real world experiences, employees lack the necessary understanding of customers and their lives to switch on empathy in their decision making.

The most effective way to understand the customer's perspective is to augment satisfaction scores with customer stories; 'walking in the customer's shoes' to experience their world from their perspective. The challenge for large organisations is scaling this across hundreds or thousands of employees.

Employees can switch on customer empathy through 'walking in the customer's shoes', using empathy tools and practices, such as empathetic listening, persona profiles, customer journey maps, service safaris and the like. Empathy tools and practices can also be used to humanise score

---

3   D. Patnaik, *Wired to Care*, New Jersey: Pearson Education, 2009, p. 99

data through attributing human qualities. Coupling the score with an emotion graph on the journey map, using photos and videos in personal profiles, linking the score with aggregated verbatim comments or spending time on the customer frontline are all examples of how this can be achieved.

Slack, the cloud-based communication software company, has institutionalised empathy as a universal value. Slack's CEO, Stewart Butterfield, believes if you can empathise with people you can do a good job, if you can't, it makes everything harder. Slack's company blog says that "for any company, empathy is a muscle, and it requires regular exercise to stay strong."

To help foster empathy at Slack, employees "spend a lot of time reading customer messages and observing customers to try to intuit what they want and need. Customer support specialists are encouraged to research the people they're helping and create mini personas for them to better understand how the customers are using Slack."[4]

Customer stories are emotionally compelling, easy for employees to absorb, easy to share and highly memorable. Most importantly, skills and tools such as empathetic listening, customer journey maps, personas, empathy mapping and the like, change the conversation from the business's performance, data points and scores, to customers' lives and are we solving their problems and making a difference.

---

4   D. Lee Yohn, '6 Ways to Build a Customer-Centric Culture', hbr.org, October 2, 2018

Power of customer stories

Stories are a part of our human evolution, they are how we learn; sharing knowledge from one generation to the next. Stories are how we remember people, places, events and experiences—they help us to connect with each other and make sense of our world. When we listen with empathy, we put ourselves in the narrator's shoes; we feel their experience—their stories connect us emotionally.

Paul Zak, founding director of the Center for Neuroeconomics, Claremont Graduate University, argues that storytelling motivates voluntary cooperation. "Oxytocin is produced when we are trusted or shown a kindness, and it motivates cooperation with others. It does this by enhancing the sense of empathy, our ability to experience others' emotions. Empathy is important for social creatures because it allows us to understand how others are likely to react to a situation, including those with whom we work."[5]

That day I asked Tim to kick off the workshop session by sharing a customer story was a moment of truth for him and the senior leadership team. They put aside their own truth of how they believed their service was being delivered to understand the customer's experience from the customer's perspective.

Tim's verbal emotional response, "I had no idea our customer experience was so poor—I AM GUTTED", and change in physical composure when sharing the customer

5   P. J. Zak, 'Why Your Brain Loves Good Storytelling', hbr.org,
     October 28, 2014

story demonstrated the power of storytelling. Customer empathy tools supported his narration and helped Tim to empathetically engage and connect his team.

In that workshop, Tim inserted himself into his customers' stories; it was as if the customer emotions that he was describing to his team jumped from him to the other people in the room. Proving that emotions can be contagious, the phenomenon was demonstrated in a study measuring public speaker anxiety and the spread of this emotion from speakers to audience members. Participants in the study, both the speakers and members of the audience, were tested for the hormones associated with anxiety. "They found that with confident speakers, the audience followed every word, feeling relaxed, but with nervous ones, the speaker's discomfort rubbed off on the audience."[6]

Storytelling is a shared experience. The best stories transport us into our customers' world—but we won't relate unless we empathise with them. The emotional impact of Tim's customer storytelling was supported by his team's willingness to listen with an empathetic ear. In Tim's case, empathy helped the team to understand the impact of the poor experiences the business was delivering.

First-hand customer stories can be confronting for employees. Listening and staying emotionally neutral from their individual beliefs, perceptions and biases, as well as from the position the business takes, is difficult. This requires humility. Some employees remain sceptical, feeling that their

---

6   F. de Waal, *Mama's Last Hug*, London: Granta Books, 2019, p. 106

efforts are being criticised or that their work is unappreciated, and sometimes they can respond with hostility.

In one such case, a senior manager questioned the validity of the research, and when I stepped him through the methodology, he retorted, "We already know these are problems." When I asked him why these problems hadn't been fixed if they were causing customer frustration, he replied, "It's on our radar, we're doing our best." It was clearly evident that this had been the case for a long time!

For other employees, customer storytelling and showing is empowering—helping to unite and align employees across the whole of the business with deep customer understanding. For many, it's an 'ah-ha' moment which makes customer satisfaction scores meaningful. Customer storytelling cultivates customer empathy in decision making and provides the evidence to create a movement for positive change—for the good of both customer and employee experiences.

Sharing the good and bad

Paul Zak argues, "When you want to motivate, persuade, or be remembered, start with a story of human struggle and eventual triumph. It will capture people's hearts—by first attracting their brains."[7] Research on the neurobiology of storytelling shows how using storytelling helps employees: "Make your people empathize with the pain the

---

7   P. J. Zak, 'Why Your Brain Loves Good Storytelling', hbr.org, October 28, 2014

customer experienced and they will also feel the pleasure of its resolution—all the more if some heroics went in to reducing suffering or struggle, or producing joy."[8]

Customer storytelling helps us to understand our customer's trials and tribulations; the customer's current state experience. Stories also engage and empower employees through sharing their contribution and efforts in improving experiences—these wins provide meaning, helping them to understand why they're doing the work and how their contribution is making a difference. "Helping others feels good. This is considered the basis for collaboration, cooperation and reciprocity in human relationships. By feeling the pain of others, we are motivated to help them, which brings about a good feeling in others, ensuring that helping behaviour is likely to be reciprocated ..."[9]

Studies show that with effort and practice, empathetic ability can be developed: "Empathy is like a habit or a skill we can learn and practice for improvement, much like reciting vocabulary over and over again or practicing in sports."[10] This suggests that by incorporating simple activities into our daily routines we can build our customer empathy ability.

For every employee to adopt a customer-centric mindset, customer stories need to be embedded in a business's day-to-day behaviour—employees need constant prompts to develop empathetic connection. There needs to be a shift from the business status quo to new practices that

---

8   Ibid

9   H. Riess, MD, *The Empathy Effect*, Boulder: Sounds True, 2018, p. 18

10   J. Zaki, *The War for Kindness*, London: Robinson, 2019, p. 50

nudge changes in how things get done: mapping customer journeys, sharing customer information and insights across employee teams, using service safaris, empathy mapping before problem solving, including a 'customer minute' in daily huddles and the like.

Case in point

Storytelling is a powerful driver of empathy. Jamil Zaki, Professor of Psychology at Stanford University and author of *The War for Kindness*, points readers to the 'Changing Lives' program implemented in some of the poorest communities in the United States. Changing Lives was the first program of its kind to integrate literature studies into the criminal justice system.

Changing Lives was conceived in the 1990s on the back of English Professor Bob Waxler's experience teaching literature, and District Court Judge Bob Kane's frustration with seeing the same people charged with the same crimes over and over again. Initially, the program was run as an experiment; eight serial offenders, including several criminals who had carried out violent crimes, joined a class every two weeks to discuss works of fiction. The classes "discouraged students from talking about their own biographies—but the characters in each story gave them a new lens through which to see themselves."[11]

---

11   J. Zaki, *The War for Kindness*, London: Robinson, 2019, p. 89

The course ran a number of times after this first experimental session. Students were encouraged to share their views and feelings about characters and situations. The men also began telling stories, not only reading them—they were learning about people's lives and as a result, Waxler believes the program instilled greater empathy in them.

The benefits of the program were tested. Researchers reviewed four of the classes, comparing students against criminals with similar demographic and criminal profiles who had reoffended. "By the end of the year, 45 percent of probationers in the comparison group had reoffended … In that same time, less than 20 percent of Changing Lives students had reoffended …"[12] The cost benefits were significant: "Changing Lives costs about $500 per student, compared to upwards of $30,000 a year of jail time if that student reoffends."[13]

Storytelling enables us to step into another person's world, helping us to better understand and feel what customers are experiencing when they interact with our products and services. While the trend in business is to utilise customer satisfaction scores as the sole measure of performance, this metric neglects the importance of connecting emotionally with customers—to humanise employee behaviours, develop customer-centric thinking and actions and strengthen communication to improve efforts in delivering customer experience excellence.

---

12   Ibid, p. 91
13   Ibid, p. 92

7
Leading
with
Purpose

They all agreed there had to be a better way to purchase glasses that didn't burn a hole in their wallets. Neil Blumenthal and the co-founders of eyewear company Warby Parker believed that "the best businesses and products solve real problems"[1] so they set about developing a solution.

Warby Parker's 'home try-on program', the first of its kind, made it possible for consumers to purchase quality frames at a fraction of the price of other retailers. As Blumenthal says, "We always try to put the customer first and ask, Does this solve a problem? Does this make something more fun and easy for our customers?"[2]

As Blumenthal tells it, when the company started it was essentially established to meet the needs of its founders and at that time one of their core values was "treat others

1   A. Wray, 'Eyewear With Empathy: Warby Parker's Neil Blumenthal', redef.com, October 20, 2015
2   Ibid

the way that *we* want to be treated."[3] However, the leadership team soon realised "that it's actually more empathetic to treat others the way *they* want to be treated, because not everyone wants to be treated the same way."[4]

Blumenthal's ambition has always been to demonstrate that a high-growth company can be profitable, provide exceptional customer value and do good in the world. Warby Parker's social mission, their purpose, is giving back to communities in developing countries by providing eyewear to the people who need it most, through their 'Buy a Pair, Give a Pair' business model. To date, the "company reports it has officially distributed five million pairs of glasses to those in need in more than 50 countries around the world."[5]

Impacting people's lives

A cause is the purpose, aim or movement to which your organisation is committed and is prepared to defend or advocate for. Companies that are recognised for customer experience excellence are an example of businesses that live their customer cause. A company's cause helps to differentiate, build a deeper stakeholder connection and drive growth.

---

3   A. Wray, 'Eyewear With Empathy: Warby Parker's Neil Blumenthal', redef.com, October 20, 2015

4   Ibid

5   'Warby Parker Reports Milestone of Distributing Five Million Pairs of Glasses to Those in Need', visionmonday.com, March 13, 2019

Customers' expectations are continuously evolving. Increasingly, customers want to purchase brands that not only provide rewarding experiences, but also reflect the type of world they want to live in. The brands that we choose now need to stand for something; using their resources for good, as well as making profits.

Procter & Gamble's Chief Brand Officer, Marc Pritchard, says, "what consumers are now expecting is brands to do good for the world as well and to go beyond just providing a superior product. They want to know what your values are. Is it a diverse group of people behind this brand? Are you promoting equality of all types, whether it be gender or race, ethnicity, sexual or gender identity, ability, even age, and religion? Are you walking the talk both with your own company and then with who you work with?"[6]

It's the same with employees. The reality is, the majority of employees end up working towards their own goals; earning a wage to support their family or to support their desired lifestyle. Many of them meander through their working lives unmotivated, unappreciated and unhappy; feeling that their employer provides little room for them to grow as individuals and that their goals are not aligned with those of the business.

Studies show employees want more that just jobs and often feel indentured to a model of work that doesn't

---

6   A. Aziz, 'The Power Of Purpose: How Procter & Gamble Is Becoming 'A Force For Good And A Force For Growth' Pt 1', forbes.com, July 16, 2019

provide meaning. Employees want to feel passionate and proud that their contribution is making a difference. They not only want to know what they're doing but 'why' they are doing it, and how they're contributing. Working with a purpose provides a sense of belonging to something greater, contributing to something bigger, something more than the business or the brand. Purpose energises employees in a way that pursuing profits alone never will.

For example, what energises and drives Warby Parker employees is their social mission; to provide glasses to people who need it most through their 'Buy a Pair, Give a Pair' business model. Neil Blumenthal says, "It's what gets us up in the morning. It's what prevents us from hitting the snooze button and spending another 15 minutes sleeping. And for our 1,800 current employees and for people that we're recruiting, we lead with social mission. That's the No. 1 reason people want to come work for Warby Parker."[7]

The leaders I talk with are often looking to connect customers and employees with their company in new and different ways. They too, have a deep yearning to deliver greater value for the customers they serve and are striving for ways to empower employees—where everyone works together for a cause that's good for customers, employees and for the business too.

---

7   C. Lagorio-Chafkin, 'Warby Parker Had a Mission. Its Customers Didn't Care. Here's How the Company Changed Its Message', inc.com, April 11, 2019

Leading with empathy, the ability to perspective-take, helps us to see different aspects of a situation and respond accordingly. Empathy expert Daniel Goleman describes how empathetic leadership, "can change the brain chemistry of both leader and followers by creating an interconnectedness of thoughts and feelings."[8]

According to Goleman, this "social intelligence" not only promotes social bonding and inspires trust, it can also "prompt followers to literally mimic" the thoughts and emotions of a leader.[9] Leaders who can meet differences with empathy, who understand themselves, learn from experiences, lead with inclusive values and use their 'heart and head' to build deeper human connections, improve their relationships at even the most difficult moments.

As Neil Blumenthal says about Warby Parker's leadership, "We want to be that example that other folks can follow. We need more business leaders to be considering the impact of their products on all stakeholders, and we need leaders to be thinking about that impact in a much more sophisticated way."[10]

I encourage company leaders to explore their individual leadership purpose as part of uncovering and living their organisation's purpose. Defining their 'why'

---

8   H. Riess, MD, *The Empathy Effect*, Boulder: Sounds True, 2018, p. 149

9   Ibid

10   C. Lagorio-Chafkin, 'Warby Parker Had a Mission. Its Customers Didn't Care. Here's How the Company Changed Its Message', inc.com, April 11, 2019

helps leaders to shift from internally focused motivations, 'It's about me' to external actions, 'What's my contribution?' Purpose-led leaders choose their path and find the courage to live it—their sense of purpose not only positively impacts the organisation's cause, it also inspires and influences others.

Proctor & Gamble's Marc Pritchard believes his own purpose journey has helped him find his voice: "I think largely because being in a position of senior leadership and being willing to express points of view or tell personal stories about myself helps create some emotional safety for others to be able to speak up."[11]

Your cause is not about the business, the brand or product and service offerings. It's about the people you serve and making a difference in their lives—the customers that use your products and services, your employees, shareholders and the wider community. This is the new world business approach that delivers high growth and profitability, provides exceptional value to customers, and does good in the world.

Start with empathy

As a leader, if you really want to know what the business stands for in the minds of your employees and customers,

---

11   A. Aziz, 'The Power Of Purpose: How Procter & Gamble Is Becoming 'A Force For Good And A Force For Growth' Pt 1', forbes.com, July 16, 2019

you will need to go beyond carefully crafted organisational statements and much further than a discussion with senior executives. Purpose exists in the people you serve; customers, employees, shareholders and the wider community.

Guiding an organisation through uncovering and defining purpose starts with deeply understanding the needs of these people to make a difference in their lives. It's vital to understand your customers' and employees' worlds, so I always ask leadership teams to begin their organisational purpose journey with a listening tour.

Start by going into the business and listening with empathy to line managers and employees—on the frontline and in the back office. Get an employee pulse; a sense of the big picture issues that are concerning them and their customers and the contribution they'd like to make.

The aim is to listen with an empathetic ear, to understand their point of view, to be curious and ask questions, and to ask yourself, 'What must this feel like?' Remain open minded and share your understanding with them. Approach this using first-hand discussions to discover the common themes; how do they feel about the work that they do, what are their passions and what energises them?

Unlike their employees, Warby Parker's customers weren't as motivated by the company's social mission. So clearly, it's just as important to continue a listening tour with customers. First-hand conversations, in-depth discussions or customer immersion sessions are effective ways to understand customers' lives from their perspective; their needs, goals and experiences, and critically, why they feel the way they do. These first-hand customer discussions are rich in insight, language and emotion; opening up unrealised opportunities.

Through listening, Blumenthal learned that his customers' needs differed from the founders' expectations. The customer goal was style and fit first: "So, fashion and design came first for us. After style and fit come value and customer experience. Third comes our Buy a Pair, Give a Pair program. While customers certainly love the fact that we give back, at the end of the day, it's not a critical factor in deciding whether to buy a pair of glasses."[12]

This is where the rubber hit the road for the Warby Parker business. Deep understanding of their customers' needs was fundamental in developing a value proposition that delivers a signature customer experience. Interestingly, this point underscores the value of customer empathy. Blumenthal could have easily clung tight to the original purpose-led proposition of 'Buy a Pair, Give a Pair', however his ability to empathise with his customers; to understand what really mattered to them and use this in his problem solving has been instrumental in developing a strong customer-centric cause.

---

12   C. Lagorio-Chafkin, 'Warby Parker Had a Mission. Its Customers Didn't Care. Here's How the Company Changed Its Message', inc.com, April 11, 2019

Perspective-taking enables leaders around the decision-making table to take into consideration employee and customer needs and perspectives; augmenting their assumptions and opinions with a different way to look at the world; helping them to remain steadfast on making a difference in people's lives.

Purpose needs action

I have found that people always have an abundance of energy and enthusiasm to do the things they care about and believe in. For leadership teams the question remains, how to draw on this and unite customers, employees, shareholders and the wider world behind the company's cause.

For a mission to have impact, purpose needs to be knitted into the fabric of a business's culture. A worthwhile cause, whether it's customer, community, societal or global, drives positive employee behaviour; shaping customer experiences, energising and uniting teams, informing the business's strategy and creating positive change.

Therein lies the challenge—the 'purpose gap'. On one side, the belief that in order to effect change, cause has to inform how the business thinks, acts and communicates. On the other side, is the organisation's capacity to do so.

The gap exists between the ideal versus the action required by leadership to operationalise the strategy, govern behaviours, develop new capabilities and ensure employee metrics and rewards tie back to the cause.

There's no quicker way to disenfranchise employees than rolling out another empty statement. I recently visited a company and commented to the receptionist that I really liked their mission and values displayed on the walls. I asked her, "What does this mean to you?" She looked up, looked back at me, and shrugged her shoulders. A telling sign that the business was perhaps built on words, and not actions.

Purpose needs action and actions need to be authentic. Authenticity is the undertaking to live the cause, with behaviours representing what the organisation values. When an organisation has purpose there's a deeper connection that informs their culture, provides a foundation for the business strategy, shapes customer and employee experiences, helps to clarify difficult decisions and builds a strong employee connection with their work.

Creating this connection between purpose and actions within the business is critical; this is where it becomes real for employees. Empathetic listening begins the process of providing shared meaning, delivering deeper connection and uniting for the cause. Employees buying into the aspiration because it's informing how they work—this is when their work becomes meaningful.

When employees line up behind and are empowered by a cause they are energised and engaged with an intent that's bigger than the business and the brand. Motivated employees inspire a sense of purpose in others and help them understand the impact they can have—they influence the right things to get done and they go the extra mile to deliver, which is good for customers, for employees and in turn, for shareholders and the business.

8
On the
Same Page

Everything that happens in our lives is a type of journey. It might be a journey that spans 30 minutes, 30 days, or an entire lifetime. It could be sitting in a cafe with a hot cup of coffee, repairing your bike, renting your first apartment, or saving for an overseas holiday.

Airbnb is a brand that's famous for disrupting the hospitality industry through connecting travellers and homeowners with the experience of home-stays and living like a local. The founders conceived the idea after turning their apartment into a bed and breakfast. Traditionally, hotels have provided a comfortable room and a nice bed; satisfying a customer's functional need. Conversely, Airbnb hosts provide the experience of being a guest in someone's home, fulfilling a customer's emotional need—the feeling of belonging.

In 2011 the Airbnb business was entering a hyper-growth stage with over a million nights booked across

182 countries.[1] Founder and CEO Brian Chesky wanted to challenge the status quo; he wanted to see the Airbnb experience from a new perspective. Inspired by Walt Disney's storyboarding, his design team set about mapping their customers' stories using customer journeys.

Mapping their customer stories was a turning point: "Suddenly, we were looking at a journey through these sticky notes, imagining our customers booking, and we saw that the moments that mattered most were offline."[2] This approach gave the team a new perspective, a new way to see the experience. "We could see completely new possibilities in how we thought about which problems to solve and what to build."[3]

The team shared the journeys with the wider Airbnb team. Asking individual team members how they impacted the customer story. "Giving people problems instead of to-do lists empowered them to examine their work through a new lens"[4]—that of their customers.

Customer stories are at the heart their company culture and strategy. "We could see completely new possibilities in how we thought about which problems to solve and what to build."[5] The customer journey provided a framework to

1   E. F. Joffrion, 'The Designer Who Changed Airbnb's Entire Strategy', forbes.com, July 9, 2018
2   Ibid
3   Ibid
4   Ibid
5   Ibid

put the customer at the centre of solving problems, imagining new experiences and innovating brand and product extensions.

Customer experience understanding

The aim of mapping the customer journey is to distill large amounts of complex data and visualise this in a simple, engaging and relevant way. Journey maps are a powerful customer storytelling tool that provide employees the opportunity to see, touch and feel what customers are experiencing.

Journey maps provide an understanding of the customer's context and are used to tell customer stories from the customer's point of view. Mapping the journey not only captures customer interactions with your brand, but also the pre and post moments in the customer's experience.

From the customer's first interaction to after their purchase has been made, these before and after moments are as important as those that occur when customers are interacting with your products and services. Their experience is the sum of their end-to-end journey, not just their brand interactions; it is this that provides the experience context.

Mapping visually details all the stages of the customer journey; each step they take, their goals, and what they're thinking, doing and feeling—their emotions across every interaction. Your customers experience highs and lows, pains and gains; the journey map shows how they navigate barriers and their work-arounds, what they are feeling and how their experience has impacted them. Customer journeys very simply and effectively communicate the experience from the customer's perspective so that it can be clearly understood by all.

From my experience, journey maps are the most effective way for everyone in the business to understand the customer's experience and their own involvement in the product and service delivery. Journeys provide employee teams clarity, through demonstrating how customer interactions fit together across each business function.

Journey mapping shifts employees from functional or departmental thinking with siloed tasks, to understanding how customers move from one stage to the next and how each of the stages are integrated. Storytelling like this, helps employees understand the role they play in delivering the experience; a critical factor in aligning siloed functions in delivering customer experience excellence.

However, many businesses mistakenly map their customer journeys from the business's perspective using assumptive journey mapping. This approach neglects fundamental customer data from a first-hand customer perspective; their behaviours, their thoughts, their language, and critically, how they feel about what they're experiencing. Mapping without the customer perspective incorrectly assumes there is only a functional relationship with the product or service delivery; that their experiences have little or no associated emotion. Critically, how customers feel is not considered relevant to their experience.

Journey into emotions

Most of the time we're not aware of our emotions, and often we can have trouble putting our feelings into words—unless there's a heightened emotional moment. Across the customer journey emotions act like a highlighter, emphasising the memorable aspects of an experience.

The customer journey switches on customer empathy, connecting employees with what's important to customers. Customer stories, their experiences, communicate customers' thinking and doing in their interaction and emphasises their emotions and the role these play in how they feel. Understanding customers' emotions helps employees feel what the experience is like for the customer; it puts them in their customer's shoes, feeling the experience from their perspective.

Whilst nothing beats having first-hand customer conversations, where tone of voice, facial expressions and gestures help employees empathise with customer experiences, running a large-scale listening program, although valuable, is also time consuming in the initial phase. In the interim, an emotion graph on a journey map is a highly effective tool for nudging customer empathy at scale.

Customer emotions on a journey map are expressed visually using an emotion graph. An emotion graph measures sentiment, i.e. how customers feel at each interaction. Emotion icons or emoticons are a pictorial representation of facial expressions indicating a particular emotion—such as a 'smiley face' emoticon to indicate happiness. Emotion icons and a graphic wave are used to show the customer's emotional highs and lows from journey beginning to end.

Telling the customer story using the customer journey map and emotion graph connects employees emotionally to how customers are feeling about their experience. Communicating customer emotions as visual language integrated with customer verbatim comments emotionally connects employees—they feel what customers are feeling, as if their emotions are contagious.

Just as we can't help feeling happy when another person is happy, or we get upset and cry when we watch a sad movie, employees can't help but feel customer emotions. Emotion graphs help customer empathy to jump from one person to another and enables employees to feel what customers are experiencing. It is empathy which enables us to feel together, taking your customer's perspective and promoting empathetic concern.

Problem-solving framework

In my work with clients, the customer journey framework is used to promote customer-centric behaviours; putting customer needs at the centre of executives' and employees' thinking, problem solving and decision making. A customer journey framework visualises the customer journey (using aggregated customer data) to produce a customer journey map, and the product and service delivery of the experience to produce a service blueprint.

Both use a human-centric approach as the experience and service delivery are *always* mapped from the customer's perspective. My approach to this work is to humanise and create meaningful connection and deep understanding. For this reason I use first-hand customer conversations (if required, I then use quantitative surveys to validate findings) to map customer journeys. I have found this is the most effective way of understanding customers' lives. Through these conversations, listening with an empathic ear and being curious, I discover a new way of looking at the customer's world.

As the Airbnb team discovered through being emotionally connected and empowered using customer stories, your "job is to be a deep, empathetic listener and to imagine ways to solve their problem. Take responsibility to create something better than the customer could have imagined. They are the inspiration, but you are the creator."[6]

As a side note: the challenge in journey mapping using customer satisfaction scores alone is that the metric reflects satisfaction with brand touchpoints only. This is problematic as the customer journey is bigger than a series of brand touchpoints and includes many pre and post interactions that impact the experience. The customer context provides the whole story. Additionally, satisfaction scores do not reflect customer emotions which are critical for empathetically connecting employees with the customer's perspective.

My approach extends to mapping the product and service delivery—the service blueprint. A human-centric approach involves internal stakeholder participation; getting cross-functional teams to work together to map the current state service delivery from the customer's experience. When cross-functional teams work side-by-side; participating, discussing, reflecting and assessing how their actions, systems, processes and the brand touchpoints deliver the customer experience, it shifts their truth; changing how they think and feel about the delivery of these experiences.

---

6   E. F. Joffrion, 'The Designer Who Changed Airbnb's Entire Strategy', forbes.com, July 9, 2018

So how can a customer journey framework be used to connect customer and culture? When I first spoke with one of my clients, (a technology services company), their overall customer satisfaction was being maintained. Their challenge was a trend of decreasing customer retention. The business believed this was due to their poor on-boarding service at the beginning of the customer relationship.

Through first-hand customer conversations; listening to their customers' point of view and mapping the customer journey and service delivery from their customers' perspective, we were able to isolate the root cause of decreasing retention. We uncovered their technical service interactions were being negatively impacted by 'up-selling' product conversations, i.e. sales conversations at times when customers needed technical expertise and advice. Customers felt these interactions were inappropriate and lacked transparency—these conversations were eroding their trust.

Customer empathy creates a positive shift in employee mindset. Listening with an empathetic ear, asking questions and thinking, 'what must this feel like?', remaining free from judgment and sharing stories—gives employees the opportunity to develop meaningful customer connection and deeper understanding. When we behave empathetically, when we feel with customers, this positively impacts our problem solving and the decisions we make that impact customers' lives.

When my client stepped into their customers' world this brought their employee teams together, galvanised leaders and employees, aligning them to what was important for their customers—focusing their energies and effort in the same direction. The customer journey framework provided them with customer context in their decision making, helping them to feel what it was like to be in their customers' shoes when technical advice was needed. It helped the team see their customers as real people, with technical issues that were causing a high level of frustration.

Simply and concisely the framework communicated how each interaction was connected, which stages presented the highest customer frustrations and delivered the evidence for where the limited resources available should be invested to make the greatest impact on value. The moments that mattered to their customers provided the evidence they needed to redirect investment, from on-boarding to the 'business as usual' journey, where customer friction was highest.

Step by step their organisational behaviours are evolving from business-centric to customer-centric. The customer journey is providing a framework to guide decisions on strategy and shape changes in their culture. Their customer needs, goals and experiences are influencing strategic planning, business function reorganisation, new product design and employee performance through empathising and understanding the customer's perspective.

Striving for better decisions

Decision making in most organisations is still primarily based on 'business-focused' problem solving, such as how to increase market share, efficiency and profitability, at the expense of customer experiences. Even with access to more customer data and greater access to better methods of analysis, decision making habits are primarily focused on solving business challenges over 'what's best for customers'.

Unconscious bias influences decision making too. Biases are shaped by our frames of reference, experiences and societal norms; helping us to filter information and make decisions quickly. Once learned, these become unconscious. Unconscious bias affects our attitudes and behaviours, causing us to misjudge people and leading us to wrongly held beliefs and poor decision making.

Layer individual unconscious bias and conventional problem solving that's primarily business focused, and team decision making gets bogged down with competing agendas, internal politics and domination by powerful personalities—and it's not difficult to see how the customer agenda gets forgotten.

If we want to humanise organisational decision making to provide experiences that solve customer problems, meet their expectations and make them feel good, then customer empathy—customer perspective-taking—needs to be embedded into the everyday decision-making process.

In my experience, customer empathy is often absent from the decision-making processes of strategy and planning, prioritisation of resources and investment, building employee skills and capabilities and structuring renumeration, rewards and recognition and the like.

Using a customer journey framework switches on customer empathy and strengthens empathy skills enabling decision-makers around the table to draw on the customer's perspective—making it possible to put themselves in the shoes of the people who will be affected by the outcomes of their decisions. Empathy in decision making asks them to consider, 'If I was a customer in this situation, what would I really care about, how would this decision make me feel, what would I be thinking and will this create value for me?'

In order to connect with the customer's perspective, to be empathetic, we have to connect with our own emotions; the place inside ourselves that recognises that same feeling. Using customer empathy in decision making often makes for uncomfortable conversations. What's being shared around the decision-making table is a perspective that may not align with the business's point of view. It has been my experience that when the leadership team takes the customer perspective into account, this provides the necessary impetus for customer-centric decision making.

Empathy provides customer connection and a frame of reference for decision makers; bringing abstract data to life and humanising problem solving. Without personal connection to the customers they serve, leaders and employees lack customer experience context, immediacy and the understanding of customer feelings that's required to make positive, future-facing decisions to drive customer-centric growth.

9
Scaling Customer Empathy

D r. Delos "Toby" Cosgrove, esteemed heart surgeon and CEO of Ohio's Cleveland Clinic, finished his address to a room of Harvard Business School students and then called for questions from the audience. In this next moment, a single question would be the start of how Cleveland Clinic, one of the largest medical centre groups in the US, with 10 hospitals and 19 medical centres, 40,000+ staff and an operating budget of $6 billion[1], would in future serve their customers.

The question was: "Dr. Cosgrove, my father needed mitral valve surgery. We know about Cleveland Clinic and the excellent results you have. But we decided *not* to go there because we heard you have no empathy. We went to another hospital instead, even though it wasn't as highly

1   J. D. Clough, P. G. Studer, S. Szilagyi, *To Act as a Unit: The Story of the Cleveland Clinic*, Cleveland: Cleveland Clinic Foundation, 2011, p. 129

ranked as yours. Dr. Cosgrove, do you teach empathy at Cleveland Clinic?"[2]

Ten days later, Cosgrove was attending the opening of a new hospital in Saudi Arabia. To mark the occasion, the Saudi King hosted a ceremony attended by members of the royal family, government officials and dignitaries. In a passionate speech, which brought tears to the cheeks of the King, the head of the new hospital said, "This hospital is dedicated to the body, spirit and soul of the patient."[3] These words, and the emotional response of the Saudi King, prompted Dr. Cosgrove to reflect further on the nature of the relationship between Cleveland Clinic and its medical staff and patients.

Through the lens of its world-class facilities and highly trained doctors, specialists, nurses and staff, Cleveland Clinic was renowned for excellence in patient outcomes. However, in light of his recent experiences Dr. Cosgrove began to question if this was enough, "was this what sick people really wanted? Was it the best, most effective, or cheapest way to do medicine?" "Doctors visualised medicine as a collection of technical skills. Patients did not."[4]

Cosgrove thought on this and wondered, what if medicine was defined from the patient's perspective, what if patient care was designed from patient experience, and

2   T. Cosgrove, MD, *The Cleveland Clinic Way: Lessons in Excellence from One of the World's Leading Healthcare Organisations*, New York: McGraw-Hill Education, 2014, p. 109

3   Ibid, p. 110

4   G. Tett, *The Silo Effect*, New York: Simon & Schuster, 2016, pp. 194-195

what would this mean for how hospitals were organised and medical services delivered? Ultimately he decided he didn't just want to reorganise, he wanted to redesign medicine—breaking down the specialist silos and challenging long-held medical conventions with a new model.

Considering this possibility, Cosgrove undertook an exercise to explore how staff at Cleveland Clinic classified and organised themselves through mental reorganisation. "Mental reorganisation can sometimes be almost as effective as structural change, particularly if those two shifts go hand in hand."[5] His first step was to change how staff saw themselves; from medical definitions of doctor and nurse to 'care givers', responsible for holistic patient care, both physical and emotional.

Then Cosgrove set to work on reorganising departments from areas of specialty, for example cardiology, to treating patients and their illnesses. "Creating new multidisciplinary institutes that handled *diseases*, (such as cancer) or body *systems*, (say the brain)—and thus forced surgeons, physicians, and others to work together in treating patients."[6] Cosgrove argued that, "A neurosurgeon might be defined as a surgeon, part of that elite tribe. Or they might be just one person working on a brain, on par with other medical staff who defined themselves as brain experts. It all depended on what perspective you took."[7]

---

5   Ibid, p. 197
6   Ibid, p. 205
7   Ibid, p. 210

Dr. Cosgrove didn't stop there, he pushed for change in areas that had been sacrosanct; re-engineering doctors' renumeration to ensure better patient cooperation between departments and minimising resource duplication in treating patients. He abolished the departments of medicine and surgery and created multidisciplinary institutes.

Through listening to patient/doctor conversations he reimagined the distinction between surgeons and physicians; arguing that patients did not ask for particular specialists but instead described their symptoms and how these made them feel. "When people were sick they did not say, "I need a cardiothoracic surgeon" or "Take me to a cardiologist." Instead they would declare, "My chest hurts," or, "I can't breathe," or simply "I feel unwell."[8] So instead, Cosgrove pushed to reorganise services based on treating specific parts of the body or broad disease categories.

In 2008, Cleveland Clinic announced that its dozens of traditional departments would be reorganised into 27 institutes such as: Dermatology and Plastic Surgery Institute, Head and Neck Institute, Urology and Kidney Institute and so on. Every effort was made to break down traditional boundaries to focus resources and collaborative effort on patient care.

As you might imagine, people were shocked. The reforms brought staff resignations, fear of job losses and general nervousness about the new direction. The

---

8   G. Tett, *The Silo Effect*, New York: Simon & Schuster, 2016, p. 195

American Board of Surgery and the American Board of Medical Specialties were alarmed; what about doctors' residencies? Insurance companies demanded an explanation because their systems were aligned with traditional hospital departments.

Five years later, in 2013, the *U.S. News & World Report* ranked Cleveland Clinic the number one ranked hospital in America for patient satisfaction whereas, prior to the implementation of Dr. Cosgrove's reforms, it had been at the bottom.[9] Another five years on, "In 2018-2019, Cleveland Clinic was ranked as the #2 overall hospital in the United States by the *U.S. News & World Report*. A total of 4,656 hospitals were considered in 12 main data-driven medical and surgical specialty areas and 4 additional specialty areas with data collated on patient safety, performance measures and complication rates. In addition, for the 14th year in a row, Cleveland Clinic was ranked as the #1 hospital in the United States for cardiology and heart surgery as a specialty."[10]

Building skills and capability

As I have noted previously, I don't describe myself as an empath, yet I have the ability to feel what another feels and I'm well attuned to other people's emotions. I've deliberately worked to switch on my empathy ability; practising

9   Ibid, p. 213
10   Cleveland Clinic, en.wikipedia.org, September 2019

empathetic listening, keeping an open mind, suspending judgement and sharing my understanding of other people's perspectives—being aware of my non-verbal communication and strengthening these skills.

Like me, there are many people in all sorts of organisations that don't possess highly developed empathetic ability. Empathy expert Dr. Helen Riess observed an empathy gap in doctor/patient communication skills where poor non-verbal communication was leading to a breakdown in the relationship. In developing her empathy tools and training to improve how medical professionals speak and listen to patients, she realised the potential benefit for other types of relationships too.[11]

The reality is, as they stand, customer experience practices are not delivering the promise of customer experience excellence. In building a customer-centric culture, organisations need to build the essential customer experience capabilities to effect organisation-wide change. These skills: research and analysis, data visualisation (such as the customer journey framework), human-centred design and problem solving with Agile methodology, need to be augmented with developing and strengthening customer empathy ability.

Switching on customer empathy and strengthening these skills equates to good business practice. Cleveland Clinic's Dr. Toby Cosgrove, hadn't forgotten that Harvard Business School moment when a student asked if empathy

---

11   H. Riess, MD, *The Empathy Effect*, Boulder, Sounds True, 2018, pp. 44-45

was taught at Cleveland Clinic. Over time he'd observed that patients really didn't know if their treating caregiver was good at their job or not. What patients did know however, was how well they had been treated—and this was the catalyst for having the organisation's 43,000 staff attend a training course on empathy.

Customer empathy skills are much like other skills—learnable, and when intentionally practised, can become a part of an employee's day-to-day behaviour. In fact, many customer experience practices can be modified to incorporate building customer empathy skills. In the chapter Switching on Customer Empathy, I give examples of these customer empathy tools and methods.

Humanising collaboration

To reiterate, being customer-centric is the practice of putting your customer needs at the centre of your thinking, problem solving and decision making. The foundation of customer centricity is customer empathy and it is teams working together and collaborating cross-functionally that deliver on customer experience aspirations.

I hear you groan—because invariably, the effort required and the frequently poor outcomes mean most employees aren't fans of working cross-functionally. Many organisations struggle to break down their silos, whilst acknowledging that collaboration is the fundamental differentiator in delivering on their customer experience goals. This is what makes the Cleveland Clinic transformation exemplary.

Through the lens of the medical profession and the business's performance, Cleveland Clinic delivered excellence. As Dr. Cosgrove considered the patient's perspective though, his view changed. Cleveland Clinic's departments were constantly at risk of losing sight of their patients' needs in the face of department goals, incentives and agendas. Whilst departments were working to optimise their contribution to the patient experience, the organisation's structure didn't support a patient-first mindset.

When Dr. Cosgrove abolished the traditional hospital departments of medicine and surgery and reorganised over 40,000 staff members into patient-aligned Institutes, he rewired the entire business around patient journeys. The new patient-centric Institutes were designed to foster collaboration between doctors, surgeons, nurses and the thousands of other specialist employees—all working together to improve patient wellbeing.

Cross-functional teams by their very nature are diverse. With differing skill sets and levels of experience, a team can be made up of employees from different organisational levels and roles; both customer facing and back office. Selecting the right team members can be a tricky business; invariably those selected have a vested interest in the decisions made by the group.

Global design company IDEO's approach to cross-disciplinary innovation has learnings that can be applied to the cross-functional team selection process. Getting the right people around the table to work together from the start can overcome the inherent challenges associated with collaboration.

IDEO attributes its success to the recruitment of what CEO Tim Brown calls 'T-shaped' employees. T-shaped employees have two characteristics. The vertical stroke of the 'T' represents the skills that enable them to contribute to the creative process. The horizontal stroke of the 'T' is the employee's disposition for cross-discipline collaboration; namely empathy for another person's perspective and enthusiasm for another's area of expertise.

Brown makes the point, when employees with only one of these individual skills are brought together, collaboration becomes problematic. "What tends to happen is that each individual discipline represents its own point of view. It basically becomes a negotiation at the table as to whose point of view wins and that's when you get grey compromises where the best you can achieve is the lowest common denominator between all points of view."[12]

There are literally hundreds of texts written on the subject of workplace collaboration; mostly recommending functional improvements to the process. For my own consulting work, I borrow from Google's approach in setting a baseline of collaborative behaviours. Wanting to understand why some teams were superior collaborators, Google

12   M. T. Hansen, 'IDEO CEO Tim Brown: T-Shaped Stars: The Backbone of IDEO's Collaborative Culture', chiefexecutive.net, January 21, 2010

studied their own internal teams, and surprisingly the outcome was not optimal team size or the most productive structure for group meetings.

Instead, what they found was "less successful teams were the ones where a manager spoke 80% of the time or more. In successful collaborative teams, everyone engaged in 'conversational turn-taking'—one of the most human things we do."[13] "In situations where only one person speaks, the others didn't feel comfortable voicing their ideas, chiming in on other peoples', or correcting their more vocal team members' mistakes. Imbalanced communication, in short, defeated the purpose of collaborating in the first place."[14]

I like to think of this as 'empathetic collaboration' and it starts by establishing an empathy baseline. Using customer empathy nudges to promote active listening, asking constructive questions, valuing others' contributions, keeping an open mind, welcoming a diversity of perspectives and building on others' ideas. Once a baseline for collaborative behaviour is established, teams can begin working together.

It is impossible for a single cross-functional team to be effective in shouldering the workload of transforming customer experiences. Good customer experience management practice ensures organisation-wide participation

---

13   C. Dillon, 'Google's Unwritten Rule for Team Collaboration', blog.idonethis.com, April 5, 2016

14   Ibid

in the change. A governance structure will likely have a cross-functional steering group with an executive sponsor or direct report to the executive leadership team.

This ensures that the customer experience program remains highly visible to the business and a customer-centric approach is applied to the business's strategy, problem solving and decision making. As CX initiatives are prioritised, working groups, often using Agile methodology, are established to deliver change. Some organisations also utilise an ambassador group; a network of CX advocates who are passionately supportive of program efforts and provide grassroots support for a customer-centric culture.

Fundamental to establishing a cohesive relationship between each of these groups is formalising the customer experience aspiration and goals. Additionally, the customer journey framework, persona profiles and communication tools will be utilised as a roadmap to guide the work.

It is absolutely critical to switch on customer empathy across and down through the business. As discussed in previous chapters, it is only when employees empathetically understand customers and their experiences; feeling what it's like to be in their shoes, that they buy into meaningfully contributing to the cause.

A new study by University of Pennsylvania and University of Houston shows, when empathy is introduced into decision making, it increases cooperation and causes people to be more empathetic. In essence, empathy fosters more empathy in employees.[15] When we look at the heart of collaboration it's an act of empathy. Helping other people feels good, and empathy promotes cooperation which is essential for teams to function effectively.

Communication cadence

Surprisingly, with all the communications tools at our fingertips, most organisations still have a vertical communication gap between executive leaders and the rest of the business. What is happening at the top of the business often gets lost in translation. Even when every effort is made, using town halls, inclusion in the company newsletter, team meetings and the intranet, messaging more often than not loses its potency.

For this reason, the marketing team is your CX best buddy. They are experts in developing effective marketing programs that create an emotional connection. Internal marketing or employee marketing is a lever to promote customer centricity with consistency over time. The aim is to develop a creative platform with a single unifying look and tone, to build awareness, nurture key messaging, broadcast customer stories and foster employee advocacy for the customer cause.

Just as important is the language used by leaders in the business. The terms of reference leaders use to

15   A. L. Radzvilavicius, A. J. Stewart, J. B. Plotkin, 'Evolution of empathetic moral evaluation', elifesciences.org, April 9, 2019

communicate are the terms the rest of the business adopts. I will often hear my clients referring to customers using abstract descriptors to identify them. In one example, the company's most important customers, Priority Customers, were identified as 'PC900'. When I asked what that meant, I was told, "It stands for Priority Customer and there's 900 of them." I had to explain that this descriptor was sending a message to employees that even the company's most important customers were thought of as just a number rather than real people with real needs and expectations— a subtle difference that makes a big cultural impact.

The language of leaders influences organisational jargon and it spreads like wildfire. How we talk about our customers shows up in the organisation's behaviour. Interestingly, customers rarely use the same business speak or industry terminology as organisations use when describing their experiences.

A classic example is defining the customer's journey using the business's language. As discussed in Chapter 8, On the Same Page, when organisations assumptively map their customer journeys they neglect their customers' perspective. In doing so, they use business rather than customer speak to communicate the experience. Using customer language; how customers think, feel and act, helps employees to meaningfully connect with and deeply understand the customer's world.

Customer empathy 'nudges' can be used to boost how employees think, act and communicate. Nudges are small and subtle prompts that can inspire employee behavioural change. A growing number of psychologists are using nudges to help people choose empathy, even when they might otherwise avoid it. To illustrate how nudge theory works, empathy expert Jamil Zaki, shared the following case study in his book, *The War for Kindness*.

As the AIDS epidemic worsened in the late 1980s and early 1990s so did the stigma attached to having the disease, with victims often blamed for their illness. Thousands of people were rapidly afflicted. "The victims were statistics, and strangers—two big reasons not to empathize."[16] Psychologist Dan Batson "knew that people naturally care about single individuals and their stories. Could he leverage that to get them to empathise with a whole group?"[17]

To test his theory he played a recording of a patient, Julie, describing the illness and her experience of living with AIDS, to a group of university students. "Sometimes I feel pretty good, but in the back of my mind it's always there. Any day I could take a turn for the worse. And I know that—at least right now—there's no escape … I feel like I was just starting to live, and now, instead I'm dying."[18]

Batson used the following empathy nudge to prompt a mindset change. He encouraged students to really listen to Julie and instructed them to imagine what this must feel like. "Unsurprisingly, this prompt increased people's

---

16   J. Zaki, *The War for Kindness*. London: Robinson, 2019, p. 43
17   Ibid
18   Ibid

empathy for Julie. But, more important, participants who imagined how Julie felt also came to care more about other people living with HIV or AIDS."[19]

Scaling customer empathy doesn't have to be complex or costly. Start with incorporating customer empathy skills into current customer experience practices. This can include: augmenting customer journeys with customer satisfaction scores, being intentional in how teams work together, developing and promoting customer listening and storytelling to ensure these skills are practised and transferable, establishing CX language, marketing the CX program internally, using empathy nudges to prompt positive behaviour changes, and establishing customer-centric rituals to ensure customers' needs are a part of employees' day-to-day thinking, actions and communications.

---

19   Ibid

10
Humanising Customer Solutions

atti Moore is affectionally known as the 'Mother of Empathy'. She is an internationally recognised industrial designer, gerontologist, professor and leading authority on consumer lifespan behaviours. When Patti was just twenty-six she undertook an extraordinary and courageous experiment.

At the time, she was working for leading design firm Raymond Loewy, the company responsible for Coke bottle and Shell logo design. During a planning meeting she asked, 'Couldn't we add a feature to the refrigerator door so that someone with arthritis would find it easy to open?'

The response from her peers was, 'We don't design for those people!' and Moore was incensed! Having been raised in the family home with her grandparents, she knew all too well the daily difficulties they experienced living in a world that didn't design for their needs.

This event set in motion her 'elder empathy' exercise in which she altered her face and body using prosthetics to disguise herself as an eighty-year-old woman with reduced mobility, eyesight, and hearing; giving her the capacity to respond to people, products and environments as an elder person.

After a three-year journey across 14 states and 116 cities, her experiential empathy research propelled her in a radical new direction in socially conscious design that aimed to solve society's problems, address people's every-day challenges and help organisations innovate to enhance customer value.

In reading Moore's story you might presume that her empathy exercise is not relevant or scalable in a business context—I can assure you that it is. There are learnings from this exercise that can be applied to improve innovation efforts in any organisation.

Lesson 1 – Thwarting biases

One of the struggles of innovating is objectivity—processing information through the lens of our own biases, frames of reference and even the behavioural norms of a business's culture, such as the assumptions we make of what will work and what won't. Our truths, the values, beliefs and expectations that we hold as individuals, influence our creative thinking and problem solving in the design process.

Patti Moore's experiences helped her to intimately understand how difficult the world was for older people to negotiate. Empathy helped her to see a different point of view—it was her ability to empathise that enabled her to better understand and feel her elder character's experiences. Moore used her learnings to make sense of their world and bring meaning to what was important; understanding them as people, as individuals; discovering their unmet needs and points of view. Empathy helped thwart her biases.

Like Patti Moore, instead of thinking about customers just as consumers or users of products and services, we need to reframe them as part of the solution—designing for unmet needs and innovating to make our customers' lives better. The customer context and perspective helps employees break free of the counterproductive mindset of delivering more conventional and often minor improvements in product and service aesthetics or features.

Designing with empathy gets employees to look at the world differently—not through their own or the business's lens, but through the lens of who they are designing for; what are their customers' aspirations and goals and how will the experience make their customers feel. We need to free our thinking from the assumptions and judgements that get in the way of ideas that are meaningful and effective and that enhance value.

Lesson 2 – Acting it out

Businesses mostly use role play as a low fidelity method of prototyping new service experiences. Role playing is a technique used to act out service delivery by stepping into the customer's world and feeling the experience from the customer's perspective. The human-centric design method gives participants, such as designers and employees, the opportunity to 'try on the experiences' which leads to powerful insights into customers.

In Patti Moore's approach to perspective-taking, she role played characters for each of her octogenarian lives. Acting as nine different women; playing the role of the very poor to the very wealthy. "She put on makeup so she looked old and wrinkly, wore glasses that blurred her vision, clipped on a brace and wrapped bandages around her torso so she was hunched over, plugged up her ears so she couldn't hear well, and put on awkward, uneven shoes so she was forced to walk with a stick."[1]

The role play method constructs characters that represent customers in particular experience scenarios. Each employee actor 'steps into a character', becoming that customer. Role playing the scenario focuses attention on the interactions between actors within the scenario; the interactions and emotions associated with the experience relate to the scene constructed.

Taking on a character and living through the customer's experience is a way of nudging empathy. Studies by psychologist Dr. Thalia Goldstein have shown that for students, studying theatre acting over a twelve-month period, "grew students' cognitive empathy over the year, whereas

---

1   R. Krznaric, 'How an industrial designer discovered the elderly', romankrznaric.com

other forms of arts did not."[2] In another study's preliminary findings, "Medical residents who train in drama interact more empathically with patients afterwards."[3]

Tim Brown, founder of design company IDEO, explains in his TED Talk, 'Tales of creativity and play', that when children play dress-ups, they take on a character's identity—the kid dressing up as a fireman wants to know what it's like to be a fire fighter; they have a willingness to explore and surrender themselves to the experience. As adults, when we role play we are doing the same thing; we are trying on the experiences. Stepping into the character of our customer creates empathy for their experience, and this leads to powerful insights about that experience.

As Brown says, "So when, as adults, we role play, we have a huge set of these scripts all ready internalised; we've gone through lots of experiences in life and they provide a strong intuition on whether an interaction is going to work. So we're very good, when acting out a solution, at spotting whether something lacks authenticity." This is why Brown considers role play to be of value in creating experiences and why, for designers "to explore role-play is to put ourselves through an experience which we're designing for and to project ourselves into an experience."[4]

As I've said previously, describing emotions using words is difficult; acting out makes expressing feelings

2   J. Zaki, *The War for Kindness*. London: Robinson, 2019, p. 80

3   Ibid, p. 81

4   T. Brown, 'Tales of creativity and play', ted.com, May, 2008

easier. Role play gives employees permission to think and feel through a character, enabling them to discuss how the customer is feeling, how the solution is impacting them and their response to that experience. This is how customer empathy positively impacts design.

For experienced service designers, role play is part of their tool box. For employee teams however, role playing can be an uncomfortable new idea. Team members can have reservations about the validity of the method; usually a symptom of their own self-consciousness and fear of being embarrassed. For this reason, facilitators need to create a safe space, so that participants can trust the process.

We can learn from Patti Moore's empathy exercise, that playing the role of customers in orchestrated scenarios helps employees understand the customer perspective—think of it as 'learn-by-doing'. They then apply the learnings, how these experiences made them feel, to their problem solving; designing solutions that feel more human and make a real difference in customers' lives.

Lesson 3 – Empathy delivers insight

Moore's experiential empathy research helped her to see a different point of view. When we look at something from a different perspective we can learn something new that we did not, or could not, otherwise have known. This is how an insight is discovered. An insight in this context is a fundamental customer need that creates value for customers and the business alike. It is customer empathy that delivers the possibility, through perspective-taking, of discovering a new way of looking at the world.

An example of 'a new way of looking at the world' is how we perceive the digital world we now live in. If you take a walk down your street, not much has really changed; the buildings, roads, cars and people are mostly the same. That's until you take a closer look, through a different lens. "The people are mostly talking to themselves, or staring at their hands, and the banks, post offices and libraries are coffee shops, because most of their functions have moved online. As a result, we rarely 'see' the digital world as it really is—even as it makes more and more claims over our lives."[5]

Seung Chan Lim is the director of Project Realizing Empathy. In his TED Talk he discusses empathy as giving us possibilities to find a new angle from which to see the world—a new angle that will be surprising, but not so obvious in hindsight. Whether that 'new angle' is through observing behaviour, first-hand customer conversations, co-creation or prototyping, customer empathy delivers insights for innovation and competitive advantage. This new angle is understanding the customer perspective to discover a new way to look at their world. For organisations this is now a strategic imperative for growth.

---

5   J. Bridle, 'New Ways of Seeing: can John Berger's classic decode our baffling digital age?', theguardian.com, April 17, 2019

11
Switching On Customer Empathy

Henry Ford once said, "If there is any great secret of success in life, it lies in the ability to get the other person's point of view and to see things from that person's angle as well as from one's own."

Focused on getting another's point of view, the modern-day Ford Motor Company introduced empathy skills training as part of their employee on-boarding program for new engineers. The empathy skills training was designed to help engineers improve their customer understanding, by having them wear an 'empathy belly' that simulates the experience of being an expectant mother.

The empathy belly is a strap-on, weighted pregnancy belly suit, that impedes mobility and causes discomfort—including back pain and bladder pressure. It even replicates the sensation of a baby kicking to help engineers feel what it's like to be pregnant and the ergonomic challenges pregnant women experience.

Engineers wear the belly to operate the vehicle; getting in and out of the car seat, reaching for and buckling-up their seat belt, adjusting the seat and mirrors and loading and unloading the boot, to experience the challenges and physical limitations that pregnancy brings when operating a car.

After 30 minutes of simulated pregnancy, male colleagues often ask Ford ergonomics specialist Katie Allanson when they can take off the belly. "Three more months to go," she jokes. "The practice has influenced ergonomic features in certain models, such as easier automatic adjustments of the driver seat."[1]

Ford's empathy program facilitated context for design using contextual cues from their customers' experiences. The program is about much more than simply rolling more cars off the production line—the company wants to meet customers' needs, understand how their vehicles affect their customers' lives and make a difference in their experience.

New organisational norms

Switching on empathy ability, learning and developing customer empathy skills and intentionally practising helps employees improve their customer centricity; putting

---

1   J. S. Lublin, 'Companies Try a New Strategy: Empathy Training', wsj.com, June 21, 2016

customers' needs at the centre of their thinking, problem solving and decision making. By practising empathetic listening, being curious and asking questions, remaining open minded and free from judgment and sharing our understanding, we develop the skills that help strengthen our empathy ability.

Creating new behaviours assists in this change. Habits form that put your brain on auto-pilot, so you can go about your day-to-day activities without having to think too much about them. Forming new behaviours requires a change in old habits. Developing new skills takes some work, however, when practised frequently over time, studies show that people develop a strong tendency to adopt new behaviours.

The list following introduces the customer-centric frameworks, methods, tools and rituals I use in my customer experience management consulting to develop and strengthen customer empathy. This selection is written to assist switching on employees' customer empathy ability to humanise customer experience management and design practice.

Asking 'What Would Our Customers Think?' or 'How Would This Make Our Customers Feel?'

This simple question is a customer-centric game changer. All too often, conventional business-biased behaviours overwhelm the process of solving customer problems. This question is a decision making ritual that asks meeting participants around the decision making table to step into the customer's shoes and consider how their thinking or the team's ideas will impact the customer's experience.

Hints

– Encourage meeting participation by explaining how it works

– Use empathy nudges to prompt, e.g. as a reminder include the question on your meeting agendas

Customer Chair

This activity is a cultural circuit breaker practice that shifts employee focus in meetings from 'business as usual' to customer-centric discussions and decisions. Amazon founder Jeff Bezos is said to use the practice of a Customer Chair to represent the Amazon customer in his leadership team meetings. As discussions are held, arguments raised and decisions made, meeting participants ask, "What would the customer think of that?"

Hints

– The chair is symbolic of the customer sitting at the decision-making table

– Encourage wide participation by explaining how it works

–   Practise to deliver a new, organisation-wide meeting norm

Customer Empathy Mapping

Empathy Mapping is an easy-to-use tool that helps employees focus their thinking on customers—enabling them to step out of their busy day-to-day business mindset and into the customer's world to focus on solving customer problems. Empathy Mapping can be applied broadly and used, for example, to kick off a team meeting, start conversations to bring common understanding quickly to diverse employee groups, and deliver shared employee experience for problem solving.

Quick Guide

–   Download and print an Empathy Map canvas for each employee group

–   Participants' thoughts are recorded on sticky notes—one thought per note

–   Participants discuss thoughts as notes are placed on the canvas

–   At the end of the session ask employees to share what they have learned

Hints

–   Find a free canvas online and print onto A3 paper

- Circulate customer Need State Persona Profiles as part of the session
- Focus mapping on points of time or specific customer experiences

Customer Listening Immersion

Customer Listening Immersion sessions are good for groups of employees. More of a longer conversation—like having a discussion with a group of friends—these sessions are powerful empathy builders, especially for non-customer facing employees and executives who have low-to-no physical connection with customers. During these sessions, employees listen to customers' first-hand stories about their experiences; feeling what it's like to be a customer and hearing their point of view to better understand their perspective.

Quick Guide

- These sessions work best outside the office environment
- Invite to customers comes from your CEO
- The listening session style is a conversation not an interview
- A three-hour session gives time to develop rapport
- At end of session, ask employees to share what they have learned

- Agree on the hypothesis of the problem to be solved

- Brief employees on good empathy listening practice

- Discussion guide is maximum five questions

Customer Listen-to-Understand Program

Take a leaf from Amazon's Jeff Bezos's book and develop an organisation-wide Customer Listen-to-Understand Program. Amazon uses listening as part of employee on-boarding and training. Each year thousands of managers, including Jeff himself, attend two days of call centre customer listening to better understand customers, their experiences and how Amazon solves their problems.

Hints

- Include customer-facing and non-customer facing employees from all levels

- Brief employees on good empathy listening practice

- At the end of the session ask employees to share what they have learned

Customer Journey Framework

A Customer Journey Framework visualises the customer journey (using aggregated customer data from first-hand customer conversations) called a customer journey map.

The framework also details the product and service delivery of the experience, called a service blueprint—both are mapped from the customer perspective. The Customer Journey Framework is utilised to align and drive company-wide focus across customer listening, storytelling, planning and prioritisation of experience improvements, new language and ways of communicating—uniting and aligning cross-functional teams with a single customer view.

Customer Minute

A Customer Minute is a short and simple ritual of customer storytelling that creates positive new behaviour. Spending just one minute a day at the start of every meeting or at the beginning of a daily huddle or stand up to share a customer story. The aim is to bring customers to the centre of the team's thinking and discussions.

Hints

– Customer Minute is a listening with empathy exercise

– Meetings commence with a customer story

– The exercise runs for one minute only

Customer Experience Room

A Customer Experience Room is a physical or digital immersion space that uses customer storytelling to engage and connect employees with customers' lives. The room includes journey mapping artefacts, need state personas, photos and videos of customer interactions, customer quotes from research, customer feedback and recorded service calls. Immersion in the customer's world helps employees step out of their busy business world and experience the customer's point of view. Customer Rooms are used for: team meetings, design workshops, exploring future state experiences, employee training, new team member on-boarding and the like.

Hints

- Seek permission from customers to use their information and ensure customers are de-identified

- Update current state experience mapping as journeys improve

- Refresh customer stories as CX program matures

Emotion Graph

An Emotion Graph is an excellent tool to help develop customer empathy—connecting employees with how customers are feeling and giving them the ability to feel what customers are experiencing. Customer emotions on a journey map are expressed using an emotion graph. An emotion graph measures and communicates emotion; how customers feel at each interaction. Customer emotions expressed as feelings are illustrated using visual language such as emoticons and a graphic wave that shows the customer's emotional highs and lows from journey beginning to end.

Hints

- Utilise validated qualitative customer research

- Focus on an end-to-end journey not the customer lifecycle

- Show and tell the customer story—go deep and wide across the business

Empathy Nudges

Customer Empathy 'Nudges' are used to boost how employees think, act and communicate. Nudges are small and subtle prompts that can inspire positive behavioural change in employees. By definition, empathy nudges should be easy and inexpensive to implement. Good customer nudge examples include: persona profile decals, a vacant chair that symbolises the customer in meetings, customer 'storytelling minute' at the start of meetings, starting brainstorm sessions with customer empathy mapping and the like.

Listening Tour

Listening Tours are a way for organisational leaders to engage in employee and customer conversations to understand stakeholder perspectives. When executives listen with empathy, are curious and communicate their understanding, this symbolically 'opens the door' for employees to follow with empathetic behaviour change.

Quick Guide

–   Announce the intention to the business

–   Communicate how outputs will be used

–   Build rapport and trust before asking questions

–   Finish by asking, is there anything they'd like to ask?

Hints

–   This is not an interview, it's a conversation

–   The aim is to understand their perspective

–   Use 1-on-1 conversations rather than stakeholder groups

–   Keep discussions to thirty minutes

Need State Customer Persona

Customer Personas are developed from validated qualitative and quantitative data representing your customer segments—they provide a crystal clear picture in the minds of employees of who their customers are and what's important to them. A Need State Persona should feature your customer's goal and their needs: functional, emotional and social, as well as their behaviours and moments-of-truth. Proto-personas are a variant of a persona. Based on assumptions and originating from brainstorming sessions they reflect the business's beliefs about purchasing motivations.

Hints

– Make Personas highly visible to all employees

– Focus on high-value customer segments first

– Combine with customer journeys for powerful storytelling

Role Play

Role Playing is acting out the service or projecting into the experience and is used as a low fidelity method of prototyping to step into the customer's world and feel the customer's experience from their perspective. The method constructs characters that represent your customers and particular customer experience scenarios. Employees 'step into a character'; becoming the customer and playing out the experience. Role playing the scenario focuses attention on the interactions and emotions associated with the experience.

Quick Guide

– Prepare scenarios and character scripts

- Discuss session guidelines to create a safe space

- Use customer empathy mapping and storytelling to step into the customer's world

- Replay the same scenario by changing roles or with different actors

- At the end of the session ask participants to share what they have learned

- A sixty-minute session is ideal for participants to remain energised

Hints

- Role play is an excellent tool for switching on customer empathy

- Supply simple costumes to help your team get into character

- Debriefings focus on 'how the experience made them feel'

Service Safaris

Service Safaris are a holistic practice of investigating the service experience to develop an understanding of how services are delivered. A Safari is an experiential method of 'walking in the customer's shoes'; experiencing each step in the journey as your customers would. Steps can include: researching the offering, interacting with physical touchpoints, using the product or having a customer service interaction. I recommend customer journey mapping is undertaken prior to undertaking this exercise to establish the experience stages, goals and steps from the customer's perspective.

Quick Guide

– Use camera and video to document experiences

– Review stages and steps in the customer's journey

– Get out and about and experience the service delivery

– Complete the exercise with a team workshop to share observations

– Map the service delivery from the team's perspective

Hints

– Mix teams with customer-facing and non-customer facing employees

– Work in pairs to enable work in progress discussions

– Provide pairs with diaries and cameras to record the experience

– Debriefings focus on 'how the experience made them feel'

Virtual Reality (VR) Empathy Training

Virtual Reality (VR) creates virtual experiences, giving employees the ability to empathise with the customer in the scenario. VR Empathy Training helps employees step into the customer's world; feeling the experience from their perspective and making training more realistic. These scenarios help employees to bring meaning to what is important in customers' lives. VR standardises training, localises and delivers consistency and delivers intelligence on new ways to improve service experiences.

12
Bringing It All Together

I n the Prologue I posed the questions: Why, with so many organisations investing vast amounts of energy and effort into customer experience excellence, is there at best, only incremental gain? What's missing from current customer experience management and design practice that's impeding progress? How might we change the status quo to benefit customers, employees and businesses?

As it stands, customer experience management and design is overdue for radical intervention.

Meaningful connection with our customers is diminishing. We are now bound in our day-to-day work through technology, data, scores and business outcomes. Organisations are still structured to deliver greater productivity and efficiency, increasing internal competition and decreasing collaboration and communication. In consequence, businesses' thinking, problem solving and decision making have become less and less human.

Conversely, customer experiences are inherently human. Experiences are how we feel and what we remember; they are the key moments in our lives and the basis for the stories we share. The experiences we have shape our attitudes, thinking and behaviour. How we interact with the brands we bring into our lives, our customer experiences, impacts how we feel and makes a difference to our world.

Customer experiences are a complex journey of interactions and emotions that arise from customers solving problems, interacting with touchpoints, products and services and finding ways to get the job done. Customer journeys are more complex than can be measured using numbers on a spreadsheet, quantitive data and satisfaction scores alone. Understanding customer emotions during this complex journey requires switching on and strengthening our customer empathy ability.

Employees need to be given the opportunity to 'walk in their customers' shoes', to understand their point of view, to feel what customers are experiencing and consider this in their decisions. Customer emotion is the layer of evidence that provides employees context and meaning—thwarting the unconscious bias that causes poor problem solving outcomes and poor decision making—decisions that impact customer value creation, brand differentiation and sustainable growth.

Throughout the book I have discussed many ways to switch on customer empathy that will enable you to augment your current CX management practice. In my experience, journey mapping from your customers' perspective is the ideal empathy tool to deliver customer connection at *scale*. Journey maps are a powerful customer storytelling tool that provide employees the opportunity to see, touch and feel what their customers are experiencing.

Using visual language such as emotion graphs, emoticons and customer verbatim comments, journey maps express through customers' own words what they're thinking and feeling at every step and at each stage in their journey. Storytelling connects employees emotionally with the experience from their customers' perspective; promoting the development and strengthening of the three core skills of customer empathy: active listening, deep curiosity and customer storytelling.

My aim here is to humanise customer experience management and design practices by switching on customer empathy. Understanding your customers' perspective; seeing their world differently creates more meaningful customer connection, aligns and unites employee teams and enriches decisions to make a difference in customers' lives.

At the forefront of my mind was inspiring and empowering leaders with new possibilities and providing teams with customer-centric frameworks, methods and tools to leverage the most under-utilised and powerful human resource in business today—customer empathy.

Bibliography

Allwood, A. Alex Allwood website, www.alexallwood.com.
au

Aziz, A. 'The Power Of Purpose: How Procter & Gamble Is
Becoming 'A Force For Good And A Force For Growth'
Pt 1', forbes.com, July 16, 2019

Berger, W. 'Einstein and questioning: Exploring the mind
of one of our greatest thinkers', amorebeautifulquestion.com

Berger, W. 'The Power of 'Why?' and 'What If?'',
nytimes.com, July 2, 2016

Bridle, J. 'New Ways of Seeing: can John Berger's classic
decode our baffling digital age?', theguardian.com,
April 17, 2019

Brown, T. 'Tales of creativity and play', ted.com,
May, 2008

Clough, J. D., Studer, P. G., Szilagyi, S. *To Act as a Unit:
The Story of the Cleveland Clinic*, Cleveland: Cleveland
Clinic Foundation, 2011

Cosgrove, MD, T. *The Cleveland Clinic Way: Lessons in Excellence from One of the World's Leading Healthcare Organisations*, New York: McGraw-Hill Education, 2014

De Waal, F. *Mama's Last Hug*, London: Granta Publications, 2019

Dillon, C. 'Google's Unwritten Rule for Team Collaboration', blog.idonethis.com, April 5, 2016

Elliott, J. Jane Elliot website, www.janeelliott.com

Forrester website, www.forrester.com.

Gladwell, M. 'The Tipping Point', gladwell.com

Gourguechon, P. 'Empathy Is An Essential Leadership Skill – And There's Nothing Soft About It', forbes.com, December 26, 2017

Hansen, M. T. 'IDEO CEO Tim Brown: T-Shaped Stars: The Backbone of IDEO's Collaborative Culture', chiefexecutive.net, January 21, 2010

Joffrion, E. F. 'The Designer Who Changed Airbnb's Entire Strategy', forbes.com, July 9, 2018

Krznaric, R. 'How an industrial designer discovered the elderly', romankrznaric.com

Lagorio-Chafkin, C. 'Warby Parker Had a Mission. Its Customers Didn't Care. Here's How the Company Changed Its Message', inc.com, April 11, 2019

Lakas, J. M. *To Obama, With Love, Joy, Hate and Despair*, London: Bloomsbury, 2018

Lee Yohn, D. '6 Ways to Build a Customer-Centric Culture', hbr.org, October 2, 2018

Lublin, J. S. 'Companies Try a New Strategy: Empathy Training', wsj.com, June 21, 2016

McConnell, G. 'Face of empathy: Jacinda Ardern photo resonates worldwide after attack', smh.com.au, March 18, 2019

Parmar, B. 'Which Companies Are Best at Empathy?' weforum.org, December 3, 2015

Patnaik, D. *Wired To Care*. New Jersey: Pearson Education, 2009

Patten, S. 'Clubby directors in "bubble of sweet content" have no understanding lack of customers', afr.com, December 5, 2018

Paul, P. 'With Botox, Looking Good and Feeling Less', nytimes.com, June 17, 2011

Portigal, S. *Interviewing Users*, New York: Rosenfeld Media, 2013

Qualtrics website, www.qualtrics.com

Radzvilavicius, A. L., Stewart, A. J., Plotkin, J. B. 'Evolution of empathetic moral evaluation', elifesciences.org, April 9, 2019

Riess, MD, H. *The Empathy Effect*, Boulder: Sounds True, 2018

Robertson, E. 'Richard Saul Wurman, My World is a Lattice', the-talks.com, October 22, 2014

Sachdeva, S. 'Ardern advances a kinder worldview on world stage', newsroom.co.nz, September 28, 2018

Safdar, K., and Pacheco, I. 'The Dubious Management Fad Sweeping Corporate America', wsj.com, May 15, 2019

Schmidt-Subramanian, M. 'Customer-Obsessed Companies Embrace Metrics Differently', cmo.com, November 21, 2017

Seppala, E. 'Does Your Voice Reveal More Emotion Than Your Face?' greatergood.berkeley.edu, June 19, 2017

Solomon, L. 'Becoming Powerful Makes You Less Empathetic', *Empathy (HBR Emotional Intelligence Series)*, Boston: Harvard Business Review Press, 2017

Staley, O. 'United's CEO admits the airline had an unhealthy obsession with rules', qz.com, June 19, 2018

Tett, G. *The Silo Effect*, New York: Simon & Schuster, 2016

'Warby Parker Reports Milestone of Distributing Five Million Pairs of Glasses to Those in Need', visionmonday.com, March 13, 2019

Wikipedia entry, Cleveland Clinic, en.wikipedia.org

Wikipedia entry, United Express Flight 3411 incident, en.wikipedia.org

Wood Brooks, A., and John, L. K. 'The Surprising Power of Questions', hbr.org, 2018

Wray, A. 'Eyewear With Empathy: Warby Parker's Neil Blumenthal', redef.com, October 20, 2015

Zak, P. J. 'Why Your Brain Loves Good Storytelling', hbr.org, October 28, 2014

Zaki, J. *The War for Kindness*, London: Robinson, 2019

About the Author

Alex Allwood is the founder and Principal Consultant of the customer experience management consultancy, All Work Together. Alex works with leading Australian and international organisations to connect customer and culture; empowering leaders and employee teams to work together to enhance customer value and drive customer-centric growth. Alex also teaches people in business how to develop and strengthen customer empathy skills to improve their customer experience capabilities. *Customer Empathy* is Alex's second book. You can find more of her writing in local and international publications.

Connect with Alex Allwood

Lightning Source UK Ltd.
Milton Keynes UK
UKHW020413140921
390508UK00007B/592

9 781925 921656